AN ARTS FOUNDATION COURSE

UNITS 7, 8 AND 9 INTRODUCTION TO MUSIC

Prepared by Donald J. Burrows, Richard Middleton and Bill Strang for the Course Team

The Open University

Cover: The Handel Festival in the Crystal Palace (*Illustrated London News*, 8 July 1865)

The Open University
Walton Hall, Milton Keynes
MK7 6AA

First published 1986. Reprinted 1988, 1989, 1990, 1991, 1992, 1994

Designed by the Graphic Design Group of the Open University.

Printed and Bound in the United Kingdom by Page Bros, Norwich

ISBN 0 335 11987 5

This text forms part of an Open University course. The complete list of units in the course appears on the back cover.

For general availability of supporting material referred to in this text, please write to Open University Educational Enterprises Limited, 12 Cofferidge Close, Stony Stratford, Milton Keynes, MK11 1BY, Great Britain.

Further information on Open University courses may be obtained from the Admissions Office, The Open University, PO Box 48, Walton Hall, Milton Keynes, MK7 6AB.

1.7

PREFACE

Students usually come to the *Introduction to Music* units with widely varying experiences of music. Some of you will no doubt think that you 'know nothing about music', while others may have a very specialized experience of one area of the musical repertory – jazz, perhaps, or hymn tunes. Most of you probably fall between the two, having had casual contact with several areas of music at different times. For the purposes of this introduction we have not assumed any previous knowledge of music on your part, though we also believe that the study material will prove valuable to those who might already regard themselves as 'musicians'.

Our principal aim in these units is to suggest positive ways in which you can listen to and discuss music. Some of you may find this a difficult activity to face, perhaps because you have the idea that music is in some way mysterious and unapproachable. There may be a sense in which this is true, but there is also much about *all* music that can be studied and discussed critically, in factual and concrete terms. It is as reasonable to study a piece of music as it is to study a picture or a poem. Such study does, however, require some listening skills, and these units have a considerable emphasis on listening exercises to help you to develop these skills.

The material in the three units has been planned as a progressive course of study, and the later parts rely on you having worked thoroughly through the exercises in the earlier parts. So please be careful not to miss anything out. This Introduction requires you to use cassette examples *together with* the course units, so make sure that you have the tape to hand and – perhaps most important of all – try to organize your study time to allow for concentrated listening. This applies particularly to Unit 8 Part I, most of which is to be found on cassette, but *all* of the units include some essential cassette examples. Three television programmes and a radio programme are also linked into the themes of the unit material as an essential part of the study programme. For your reference, here is a general survey of the *Introduction to Music:*

Unit 7 (Week 1) The Nature of Music

Here we consider the characteristics of the activity people call 'music', and some of the ways in which these characteristics can be understood and talked about. In television programme 7 *What is Music?* and radio programme 4 *Musical Style* many of these questions are pursued further.

Unit 8 (Week 2)

This comprises two parts:

Part I *Listening to the Elements of Music* This explores the use of rhythm, melody, harmony, texture, timbre, dynamics and form through various musical examples recorded on cassette 3. Most of this section is to be worked from the cassette, as aural exercises, but don't forget to refer to the unit material where appropriate as well.

Part II *Syntax and Structure: Elements Become Language* Here we examine how a composer combines the various elements that were dealt with in Part I, taking a couple of short piano pieces by Schumann as examples.

Unit 9 Composer and Audience (Week 3)

This introduces you to music from two of the largest and richest musical *genres*: symphony and oratorio. As the title suggests, the musical case studies in this unit will be approached as 'compositions' and also in relation to the historical environments in which they were originally created. Two television programmes accompany this material. In television programme 8 *Composers and Audiences: Tippett and Sondheim*, two contemporary composers working in contrasted musical *genres* and styles relate their experiences of the process of composition, and comment on their perception of the composer/audience relationship. Television programme 9 *Handel's Messiah* supplements one of the major case studies in the unit by investigating the evidence for the work's composition and its development through the composer's performances.

As with the other discipline introductions, this section of the course culminates in a TMA.

The arrangement of Units 7–9 as three separate weeks' work in the scheme given above should not be regarded as rigid. We have intentionally varied the types of activity throughout these units to give you experience of some of the skills that can enrich musical studies. Some of you may find the general basic discussion of the nature of music in Unit 7 difficult to grasp; others may find this straightforward, but the listening exercises in the later units hard. Some may find the contact with the literature of 'great music' in Unit 9 particularly attractive, while others may initially feel a little timid about this. It is important to keep the development of your own skills in balance. Don't skimp on the exercises because, superficially, some parts of them come easily to you: with the listening exercises it usually pays to hear the music several times, in just the same way that it is beneficial to re-read closely-argued discussions. On the other hand, there is no need to hold back if you feel that you have mastered one section quickly: you may find the next section or unit more difficult, and it may well repay the extra time that you have 'saved' earlier on.

Whatever your individual pace through the varied materials of this *Introduction to Music*, we have written these units in the belief that three weeks' stimulating and enjoyable work lies ahead of you!

BROADCASTING

Television programme 7 *What is Music?*

Television programme 8 *Composers and Audiences: Tippett and Sondheim*

Television programme 9 *Handel's Messiah*

Radio programme 4 *Musical Style*

CASSETTE

Cassette 3, sides 1 and 2

Unit 7

THE NATURE OF MUSIC

Prepared by Richard Middleton for the Course Team

1 WHAT IS MUSIC?

You probably have an idea what the answer to that question is – even if it only takes the form of a list, a catalogue if you like, of the kinds of experience you would include under the heading 'music', and those which you would exclude. Most people, though they may not try to work out a precise definition, 'know' in an intuitive way what music is – or isn't; in fact, refusal to admit something to the category can often be the more common way of marking its boundaries (as with the parents whose reaction to their children's liking for Elvis Presley, or the Rolling Stones, or the Sex Pistols, was 'that's not music'). But *could* you put your intuitions into a more precise form? What qualities are essential before an activity or an experience can be described as musical?

Exercise

In two or three sentences try to describe what music is.

Comments

You may have approached this in various different ways. Perhaps you used the word 'sound', or related words like 'listen' or 'hear'. Perhaps you referred to 'singing' or 'playing instruments'. Perhaps your tack was through the notion of 'art': music, you may have written, is one of the arts – in which case you may have mentioned such words as 'beauty' or 'pleasure'.

Whatever your approach, I would be surprised if you didn't find it difficult to be both precise and comprehensive. To make the point about the diversity of possible approaches even clearer, here for comparison with your description is a selection of descriptions, deriving from a variety of historical periods and cultures.

1 When you are content, you sing; when you are angry, you make noise. When one shouts, he is not thinking; when he sings, he is thinking. A song is tranquil; a noise is not.
(aphorisms of the Basongye tribe of the Congo)

2 Every fresh dance or song is believed to have been first heard by hunters during their expeditions in the jungles, and attributed to forest spirits.
(report of the Asaba tribe of Nigeria)

3 Music... [is] something which is *not to be listened to in itself*... Never will it become personal, or contain an emotion. At a ceremony its presence is as necessary as incense, flowers and offerings... Here a *state of music* is required for a certain length of time, nothing more.
(description of music in the Indonesian island of Bali)

4 Music is the pleasure the human soul experiences from counting without being aware that it is counting.
(Gottfried Wilhelm Leibniz (1646–1716), German philosopher)

5 The musician of genius encompasses the entire universe within his art. He paints his pictures in sound; he makes the very silence speak; he expresses ideas by feelings and feelings by accents, and the passions that he voices move us to the very depths of our hearts.
(Jean-Jacques Rousseau (1712–78), French philosopher)

6 Music is a higher revelation than all wisdom and philosophy... Music is the mediator between intellectual and sensuous life... music is the one incorporeal entrance into the higher world of knowledge which comprehends mankind but which mankind cannot comprehend... Every real creation of art is independent, more powerful than the artist himself and returns to the divine through its manifestation.
(reported remarks of Ludwig van Beethoven (1770–1827), German composer)

7 Music is nothing other than a phenomenon of speculation... The elements at which this speculation necessarily aims are those of *sound* and *time*... All music is nothing more than a succession of impulses that converge towards a definite point of repose. (Igor Stravinsky (1882–1971), Russian composer)

8 That's what music's all about, messing with people's heads... Man, we don't know what we're doing but we can tell that it's working when we get up in front of all these people... I just play my guitar and we all play together and tunes come into our heads and we do 'em but it's nothing you can talk about, it just happens when we get there. (Jimi Hendrix (1942–70), rock musician)

9 Music is sounds, sounds heard around us whether we're in or out of concert halls... There is no such thing as an... empty time. There is always... something to hear. In fact, try as we may to make a silence, we cannot... Until I die there will be sounds. And they will continue following my death. One need not fear about the future of music. But this fearlessness only follows if, at the parting of the ways, where it is realised that sounds occur whether intended or not, one turns in the direction of those he does not intend... In musical terms, any sounds may occur in any combination and in any continuity.
(John Cage (b. 1912), American composer)

Though you can take various permutations of those accounts and find features in common, what strikes me most forcibly is their diversity.

So far we have been thinking about *concepts* of music. If we turn our attention to what music *sounds like*, the impression of diversity would be equally strong. Listen to the four short examples on cassette 3, side 1, band 1. I think you will agree that they all sound very different from one other. You may have been unsure whether the first two *were* music. The second certainly comes from a definite piece, whose composer and performers consider it music (presumably those who go to concerts to hear it do too). The first doesn't come from a piece, though it could have done: it was produced on a synthesizer, and plenty of electronic music contains similar effects.

Of course, another way of making the point about the diversity of types of music would be to suggest that you do a few days' concentrated listening to BBC Radios 1, 2 and 3. In addition to the popular songs and 'classical' music which make up the everyday diet for most of us, you might well have heard examples of non-European musics, avant-garde works or archaic-sounding folk songs, medieval music or free jazz; and you would have been in no doubt about the immense range of musical forms, techniques, sounds and effects that exist. In the age of recordings, it has become impossible to believe there is only one sort of music – and difficult to believe that one sort is *better* than others.

Another thing that strikes me about the list of quotations I have given is the oblique way in which they often tackle the problem. Rather than providing a strict definition, they tend to focus on what music does (its effects), what its purpose is (its functions), what it relates to (emotion, mathematics, philosophy, ceremony) or is different from ('noise', for example), how it comes into being (divine generosity, 'speculation', 'just playing'). Again there's a wide range.

Exercise

Let's take just one of these – function. Make a list of as many different functions of music as you can. Often these will be associated with different *contexts* – the situation or place in which the music happens.

Comments

These occur to me (you may well have others): entertainment; self-expression; aesthetic pleasure (concerts); as part of ritual and liturgy (churches and other sacred places); in conjunction with dance (dance-halls, theatre, discos, outdoors); supporting words, in song; supporting drama (opera, movie or TV soundtrack);

background (supermarket, restaurant, airport, car); ameliorating work (work songs, on the one hand, piped music in factories, on the other); assisting play (nursery rhymes); stimulating solidarity (political and military songs, national anthems); acting as signals (talking drums, fanfares).

Given this vast diversity – of definitions, types and functions – and given that all of these categories are claimed as music by at least one social group – even if others disagree, and even if the given social group disagrees about other categories – we are driven to wonder if a single, coherent definition of music is possible at all. We have to acknowledge, I think, that music is not just *there*, a universal resource – like air or water – which different cultures and social groups simply draw on. On the contrary, the phenomenon of music is culturally constructed; by that I mean that both the concept and the practice of music develop within, and as part of, the systems of behaviour, thought and value we call culture. (I'm thinking of 'culture' here in a sense somewhere between the first and second definitions in Unit 3 (section 4). Thus I see the nature of music as having to do with the anthropological 'whole way of life' of a society – the 'total network of human activities' – but with a focus on those aspects particularly concerned with meaning, symbolizing, making sense and order – the 'artistic and intellectual products and activities'.) Moreover, this phenomenon called music is constructed by different cultures according to different conventions; music is what a given culture, social group or historical period agrees to call music, while conversely one culture's music can be another's 'aural wallpaper' or 'primitive caterwauling'. Only if we recognize this element of *relativism* can we move on to a more analytical definition that is sufficiently broad to have some claim to universality. An Italian scholar, Gino Stefani, has suggested that music can be 'any type of activity performed around any type of event involving sound'. That's *very* broad, isn't it? Moreover, it's still a bit fuzzy, for it would seem not to exclude speech; but then, a good deal of music does include words, and there are 'musical' elements in speech, aren't there? So perhaps that is a vague boundary.

2 MUSIC AND SOUND

Stefani's enormously broad definition has at least three virtues. First, it is sufficiently elastic to accommodate the diversity of ideas about what music is. Secondly, it insists that music has to be made and experienced: there is *activity*, there are *events*, not just *things* (pieces, tunes, etc.). Thirdly, it notes that despite all the diversity there is at least one common feature: *all* music – I think we're safe in saying – uses *sound*. This is true even of John Cage's so-called 'silent' piece, *4′33″*, which you hear in television programme 7 *What is Music*? I suppose one can imagine an avant-garde musician inventing 'conceptual music', though I don't think it has happened yet; and for theorists of Classical Greece and Rome, and of the Middle Ages, music was so much bound up with mathematics that its highest form, *musica mundana*, comprised not only the 'music of the spheres', which sounds but is unheard by us, but also the organization of the elements and the alternation of the seasons. But let's at least say that sound is *central*. So, what is sound?

Sound is – we often think – somehow intangible, ineffable, mysterious. You can't touch sounds, as you can physical objects, or see them, as you can actions. In a sense, this is simply to say that what we call sound exists *inside* ourselves; sounds happen in human consciousness in association with certain events in the human hearing and nervous systems; there's no sound until we hear it. But, of course, these sensations are *connected* with things that happen *outside* us. Sounds are effects of external stimuli. Let's start with the outside end of the system, since we know rather more about it.

2.1 VIBRATION

Sounds are the subjective effect of the impact on the ear of *vibrations*. Any physical object or medium can be the source of such vibrations. In musical performances, what usually happens is that some *instrument* is set vibrating, the vibrations are picked up and transmitted by the surrounding air, and eventually impact on the ear. Whether you see a violinist bowing a string, a guitarist plucking one, a singer breathing through vocal chords and mouth cavities, a brass player blowing through shaped mouth and lips, or a percussionist hitting skin or metal or wood with hand or stick: in all these cases, that's what's happening.

2.2 FREQUENCY AND PITCH

The speed or *frequency* of the vibrations needs to be within a certain range (above about 20 per second and below the 16–20,000 area, with variations for individuals and for age); below the lower limit and above the upper we don't hear these as sound. The sounds most commonly used in music result from *regular* patterns of vibration; that is, the particles (of air, skin, wood or whatever) vibrate in a certain pattern which is repeated, at a steady speed. Thus we can speak of a sound having a frequency of, say, 440 cycles per second (or *Hertz*). That objective phenomenon is related to the subjective sensation we call *pitch*. The faster the vibrations, the higher the sound appears to be. A steady vibration of 440 Hertz produces the pitch to which today's 'classical' musicians usually tune before a performance. In our society the most common 'scientific' distinction between musical sound and noise (though in fact it over-simplifies the situation somewhat) is based on the idea that noise doesn't have a regular pattern of vibration.

An important phenomenon is that relationships between some musical sounds of different pitch fall into mathematically simple patterns. If we double our 440 vibration, so that we have a frequency of 880, the resulting sound will be an *octave* higher. The word 'octave' describes the sensation that two pitches are 'the same but different', as when men and women sing the same tune; if you sing the first line of 'Somewhere over the Rainbow', your first two sounds ('Some-where') comprise an octave. If we increase the 440 by half, to 660, so the ratio is 3/2 rather than 2/1, we produce a different 'interval', a *fifth*; sing the opening of 'Baa Baa, Black Sheep' and the gap or 'interval' between the first two notes and the third note ('Baa Baa → Black') is a fifth. As we reduce the ratios (4/3, 5/4...), we produce ever smaller intervals. You can derive the pitches to form a complete scale this way (classical and mediaeval theorists did). More important, it seems that in virtually every music culture the octave is fundamental; often the fifth is too.

2.3 LOUDNESS AND TIMBRE

Sounds not only have pitch: they have *loudness*; and they have *timbre* or sound quality (i.e. a violin 440 sounds different from a trumpet 440). Loudness is related to the *magnitude* of vibration: if you imagine each particle vibrating back and forth, the further it moves, the louder the sound. Timbre is related to the fact that almost all sounds are *composite* sounds; that is, within the recurring pattern of vibration, there are subsidiary frequencies as well as the fundamental frequency – so there are subsidiary pitches (or *partials*) present as well. In most musical sounds, the relationships between the partial frequencies and that of the fundamental pitch fall into the same simple ratios (2/1; 3/2; etc.) as do the intervals described before. Usually you don't hear the partials as separate pitches; what they do is add 'colour'. The particular blend (which ones are present, in what strength) is related to the quality or timbre of the total sound.

2.4 RHYTHM

If we slow down the frequency of vibration, through the lower 'pitch threshold' (around 20 Hertz), we lose the sensation of pitch. The vibrations begin to register themselves as separate pulsations; they're turning into – into what? Into *rhythm*. These separate pulsations, if their frequency remains regular, produce the effect we generally describe as a *beat*; in most music, the speed of the beat (the *tempo*) is somewhere between one and three pulses per second. Now rhythm and beat aren't the same. Beat is a regular pulse; rhythm covers the entire field of the durations of sounds, and the relationships between them. Musical use of rhythm is immensely varied. In some music, rhythm may be little more than a repeated pulse but in other music it may be a complex combination of different durations; occasionally it's hard to hear any recurrent unit of duration at all. Nevertheless, it seems to be the case that in virtually every music culture regular pulsation is important. And just as the sensations of pitch and interval can be related to physical patterns of wider applicability, expressed in mathematical proportions, so it's hard not to make analogies between pulse in music and other periodic movements: breathing and heartbeat; walking and other repetitive actions; perhaps repetitive patterns of electrical brain activity. I'm not suggesting cause and effect here; it seems to me more likely that the ways human beings structure their actions and sensations are mutually influential, that they 'interpret' each other – in interaction with our awareness of basic physical data (left/right; breathe in/breath out; etc.).

2.5 CULTURAL USES OF SOUND

I have wanted to stress the physical sources of 'sound' because of the unfortunate tendency to regard music as somehow 'airy-fairy' – less concrete than putting paint on a canvas or writing words on a page. The materials from which music derives are exactly that: materially real. Nevertheless, it's important then to go on and emphasize that *music and sound aren't the same.* What people call music isn't the physical events of vibration, and it isn't, in any blanket sense, what we hear. The sounds have to be *organized.* Thus the concept of music is a *cultural* concept and the practice of music is a *cultural* practice. Music is *related* to the physical and neuro-psychological events, but it's not *reducible* to them. Particular music cultures (we could use the plural now and say 'particular *musics*') *select* from the available spectrum of sounds, according to their own conventions. These selections vary historically and from culture to culture. They may use different scales (a scale is the collection of available pitches used in the music); they may have different ideas of which sequences and combinations of pitches are permissible; they may use simple or complex, repetitive or varied, rhythmic patterns; they may be purely vocal (e.g. Gregorian chant), or use mainly xylophones and gongs (Balinese music) or admit any sounds whatever (John Cage). And so on. This is why, to put it at its simplest, Beethoven sounds different from Jimi Hendrix, Nigerian drumming from the ceremonial music of Bali, John Cage from eighteenth-century comic opera (Rousseau wrote one). And it's why the social group associated with one of these may not understand or like or tolerate the others.

It's also why the existence of musical phenomena so basic as to be apparently universal or almost so (the octave; regular pulse) doesn't, in my view, mean that they are 'natural' or intrinsic to music, rather than culturally constructed. There *are* some musics which don't use one or either of these – particularly styles of ritual or liturgical chanting; it's perfectly possible today to produce complex music electronically which deliberately avoids both. Thus the distinction between the neuro-acoustic and musical realms is crucial. The relatively direct link between them in these cases helps explain the widespread appearance of these phenomena in music, but the appearance of these phenomena, and the exact roles they play, are still dependent on cultural criteria. Two-to-one frequency ratios and regular pulses exist in nature; whether and how 'octaves' and 'a beat' are used in music is a matter for cultural decision-taking.

We have to talk about three different categories, then: physical stimulus, sound, music; and they exist on three connected but distinct levels. There is a relationship but not a one-to-one correspondence between them. I haven't space – even if I were competent – to go in any detail into the processes of hearing. What does seem to be clear, however, is that between the three levels the human hearing system interposes *filters* and *mediators* that influence how vibrations turn into sound (these are neuro-physiological mechanisms) and how sounds are heard as music, or not (these are cultural mechanisms).

A few examples of neuro-physiological mechanisms first. Frequency and pitch are closely related but they aren't synonymous. A sound of constant frequency, if increased in loudness, appears to change pitch (if it's high, it goes up, if low, down). Because our hearing apparatus is most sensitive in the middle of the frequency range, partials which are important in characterizing a particular timbre sound weaker at high pitches than at lower pitches, resulting in a change of sound quality; yet the brain is capable of identifying, say, 'oboe timbre' throughout the oboe's range. There are not only thresholds of frequency but also of speed: very fast discrete pitches blur together to sound like a continuous slide, while extremely slow sounds (say, twenty or thirty seconds apart) may separate into disconnected events. A repeated sound, which objectively is not changing in duration or loudness, will have its pulsations grouped, so that some sound accented; this grouping activity is apparently a property of the brain, which it cannot avoid exercising.

As for cultural mechanisms, the main point is that we learn how to hear, in particular contexts. The category of the octave is acquired, for instance. Small infants aren't born with an awareness of the octave's musical significance; they have to learn it. The same is true of regular pulse, as parents who have watched their young children trying to beat regular time or dance to a regular beat will recognize. At a higher level of musical organization, sequences of sounds are sampled for identifiable patterns. There's no such thing as an 'innocent ear'; we always hear in relation to conventions and expectations absorbed from other, familiar music. The start of a melody or of a rhythmic pattern establishes a sequence which we know is more likely to continue in certain ways, less likely in others. Combinations of sounds seem 'consonant' (pleasant or harmonious) or 'dissonant' (harsh); but these are culturally conditioned concepts whose meaning has changed through different historical periods, so that the same combination can sound 'consonant' at one time, 'dissonant' at another. Some scales use 'artificial' intervals (i.e. intervals not derived from simple mathematical ratios); listeners can accept this if they're accustomed to the system. Even the octave can be 'mistuned' by a surprisingly large margin and still be recognized. The most common scale in European music (doh-ray-me-fah-soh-lah-te-doh, if you know tonic sol-fa) is now, for complicated reasons, tuned so that many of its pitches are slightly 'out of tune'; but we're so used to this that it sounds 'natural'. Sounds which we might normally regard as 'noise' – a jumbo jet passing overhead, for example – could be accepted as 'musical' when used on tape in a concert hall, as part of an electronic piece.

Exercise

Section 2 contains a lot of information and I would like to be sure you have grasped the main points. Give brief answers to the following questions:

1 What property is characteristic of *all* music?

2 What is the physical source of sound?
3 What causes the sensation of pitch?
4 If you double the frequency of vibration, what happens to the pitch?
5 What causes the sensation of loudness?
6 What word describes the 'quality' of sound – for instance, its 'oboe-ness' or its 'violin-ness'?
7 What's the difference between rhythm and beat?
8 What turns sounds into music? There has to be...... of sounds in accordance with cultural......
9 Why is there no such thing as an 'innocent ear'?

Suggested answers

1 All music uses sound.
2 Vibration
3 Frequency of vibration is directly related to the sensation of pitch.
4 It rises by one octave.
5 Loudness is related to the magnitude of vibration.
6 Timbre
7 Beat is a regular pulse; rhythm is the system of relationships between sound durations.
8 Organization; conventions
9 Because we always listen in accordance with culturally-acquired knowledge and expectations.

Note. There is more discussion of pitch, loudness, timbre and rhythm in Unit 8.

3 MUSIC AND TIME

We have already seen in passing that sounds, by definition, exist in time. With rhythms, that's obvious; but pitch, too, exists as a result of a succession of *events*: vibrations. And when we come to consider *sequences* of sounds, it's even more obvious that we're dealing with a *temporal* experience. This may seem hardly worth mentioning; we take it for granted. But it has important consequences.

Exercise

Think for a moment about music in comparison with the other arts. Try to place the various arts on a 'temporality scale': temporality very important at one end, not very important at the other.

Comments

Temporality seems least important to the visual arts. Admittedly, you don't necessarily take in every detail of a painting all at once; you may scan it quite slowly. Nevertheless, it is all there, in the one instant; it's possible to get a general impression in one glance; and, it doesn't change over time, as you scan – or even if you come back for another look the next day. Much the same is true of sculpture and architecture – though of course you may need to walk round or through the object rather than absorbing it in one glance; it is, still, completely there and basically unchanging.

Similar points can be made about literature – a novel, say – though less strongly. Of course, it takes time to read, and the story will in some way or another be reporting on events occurring over a stretch of time. Still, though, the whole book is in your hands; you can look back to remind yourself, or even skip forward. With drama, and spoken poetry, time becomes of the essence; they have to be *performed* – though you might argue that in many cases written texts exist and reading them can give a substantial part of the experience.

At the far end of the spectrum we come to dance and music. In both cases performance is essential before the art can be said to exist. No-one can perceive a piece of music in its entirety because as soon as one sound is heard it vanishes, leaving only a memory; at the same time, conversely, the piece doesn't exist as a whole until every note has been heard – at which point, paradoxically, it no longer exists (except in memory). Isolated moments from the piece may be meaningless, or take on a different significance, out of their context; the meaning of the whole piece isn't complete, and can change, right up to the final sound.

You might have suggested that, like drama and poetry, music can be written down; musicians can read a musical *score*, like a book. There's *some* validity in this comparison, but with two large qualifications. First, scores (even more than books of poetry or plays) are basically *blueprints*, not texts; they instruct performers what to do. Much important information can't be notated; all performances from scores are bound to be *interpretations*. Moreover, even skilled score-readers find it hard to 'hear' complex combinations of sounds as they read, except as an approximation. Secondly, very little music is written down. Most popular or jazz musicians don't use scores – or they use very rudimentary ones, diagrams or mnemonics really. Most non-Western music has never used scores of any kind. Only for European 'classical' music – from the church music of the Middle Ages down to the concert music of today – has notation been central. In the context of world musical culture, this is a subsidiary trend (though European 'classical' musicians would argue, perhaps rightly, that it's of enormous importance). It's probably better to think of music as a *practice* rather than a set of artefacts; this may mean paying more attention to the *doing* of it, and less to a series of 'monuments' (the scores) which the 'canon' of 'great works' turns the doing into. Incidentally, many people in cultures with non-written music manage to talk about it, often in sophisticated ways, perfectly well, and so one implication is that if you can't read music and are fearful that this means you will have difficulty studying the subject, you're probably mistaken.

What effects does music's temporality have on the way it's made and the way it's heard? Thinking about time raises a lot of complex philosophical problems which I can't go into here. For music, though, there are a few fairly straightforward but important points.

Musical time is not ordinary time. What happens in the music affects how we feel the flow of time. Many philosophers and psychologists have made a distinction between 'objective' or clock time and 'experiential' or psychological time. You will be well aware that time doesn't seem to pass uniformly. When you're doing something boring (sitting on a Costa Brava beach), it drags; when you're doing something interesting or exciting (studying A102 units), it flies past. Under some conditions, of 'ecstasy', it may 'cease to exist'. Memory, too, can play tricks. 'It seems only yesterday she was in nappies'; or alternatively, 'Was it only yesterday? It seems a lifetime ago'. Within music, the sense of time seems to be more related to what happens than to the clock. A multiplicity of varied events crammed together in quick succession can give the sensation of a big stretch of time; while a more predictable, consistent passage may 'slow' time down; an expected repetition we may even, as it were, dream through. Tempo may speed up or relax our time sense. A drastic change of tempo – or of content – may 'open out' our time perspective, as though a long journey were in progress.

Recurrence of a previous theme may work differently depending on what has intervened (a lot, a little; something quite different, something similar); or depending on whether the theme recurs in the same form or changed.

Different kinds of music often treat time differently. At the extremes, there are objectively short pieces which seem long, because they're so intense and packed with unique events (some of the tiny pieces of the twentieth-century composer Webern, for instance, were described as expressing 'a novel in a single gesture'); conversely, there are long pieces which are so changeless – in some sense – that they can, to the involved listener, seem short (much jazz improvization seems to me to be of this type; perhaps the long drum pieces traditionally practised in West Africa are too). There are also long pieces that are meant to seem long: Wagner's music dramas, for instance. There are works whose openings fall into gestures so conventionalized that to a knowledgeable listener the implied symmetries enable the shape of the whole time span to be foreseen: many eighteenth-century symphonic movements are of this kind; so are many Tin Pan Alley ballads. By contrast, there are works which are 'open-ended' – based on some kind of repetitive framework, they could 'go on for ever': jazz improvization and large-scale West African drumming again. The crucial factor seems to be whether, how and where 'landmarks' appear – in the same way that two landscapes, objectively identical in area, can seem either 'open' and 'vast' or 'full' and 'intricate', depending on their internal layout. Over and above differences in sound, thirty minutes of Beethoven aren't the same as thirty minutes of Jimi Hendrix or of Balinese music.

But it's not just a matter of how the music is put together. The attention, expectations and experiences of listeners are also important. A great deal of listening concerns *remembering*, though the remembering is often subconscious. The content of this remembering activity comprises aspects of both what has gone before in the piece and what has been heard previously in other pieces, which has established conventions; and this content then conditions what is *expected*. What we *attend* to at any given moment, then, to a large extent concerns the sorting and grasping of sequences of sounds, selecting the salient points of interest which enable us to hear them as patterns, in terms of what we remember and what we expect. In other words, listeners actively form the musical present in line with their knowledge of the musical past and future.

Furthermore, this relationship between music and listener can operate at different *levels*. Listeners seem to have a sense of a 'present'. Scientific tests suggest a definition focusing on the minimum time necessary to identify the main characteristics of a sound – its pitch, loudness, timbre; this is apparently about 1/20 of a second. In a different sense I think most listeners feel some kind of 'present' in connection with a sequence of sounds which can be grasped as a whole, as it were 'now', without any need for obvious remembering; clearly this will vary in length depending on musical conventions, context and listener knowledge – but let's say up to seven or eight seconds. The opening motive of Beethoven's fifth symphony – 'da da da dah' – or the phrase 'somewhere over the rainbow' or the phrase 'she loves you, yeah, yeah, yeah' would fit this definition. It's perfectly possible to listen purely on this level, registering the succession of presents, moment by moment. But it's also possible (and more common) to *compare* each present to what has come before and what may come next; again the comparing is often subconscious. And these pasts and futures may relate at different levels. Thus there's an immediate past (which may be the same as the present or different) and there are more distant pasts (which also may be the same or different – and whose function in the time perspective will operate accordingly, as well as in accordance with their distance). At the highest level will be the experience of the time structure of the entire piece.

4 ORGANIZING TIME

One way of thinking about listening to music would be in terms of robbery: the musicians are *taking our time*. For the musicians, then, one of the major considerations in what they're doing is how they *organize* this time. Many factors are involved: tempo, rhythm, meaningful sequences of pitches (e.g. tunes); and also *musical form*. What is imposingly termed musical form or structure, and is the subject of so many intimidating textbooks, is simply the category for all the different ways of organizing time in music. Two of the most important ways are *repetition* and *contrast*. In fact, doing the same/doing something different represents a distinction which could be seen as the basis of all musical structure.

Imagine you're composing a piece – to keep it simple, let's say an unaccompanied tune. The style is, roughly speaking, that of the jigging kind of British folk dance, the kind of thing played on fiddles or concertinas. That knowledge sets limits on what you can do and establishes conventions for what you're likely to do. You play a note. Now what? Well – you have a choice. You could repeat the note; or you could do something different. Then the same situation recurs: repeat or change? At the start, your range of options, though finite because of the style conventions, is quite wide. As the sequence of notes extends, the range narrows because you start to reduce the number of likely or predictable routes in your listeners' minds. By the end, your options have probably become very narrow. Move to the cassette and let's see how this could work.

Cassette exercise

At this point you should listen to cassette 3, side 1, band 2.

4.1 INFORMATION THEORY AND VERBAL SYNTAX

The approach used in that cassette extract derives, in a very simple way, from *information theory*. Basically this sees musical organization as focused on degrees of predictability, defined by quantity of 'information'; the less predictable a sound, the more information is imparted, the more predictable, the sound, the less information it carries. And music is seen as needing to strike a balance between too much information – which causes bewilderment or frustration – and too little (at the extreme, just repetition) – which causes boredom. Of course, where the balance falls varies with several factors: style, composer, listener expertise in the style, level of listener attention, listening context, function of the piece, etc. And even then I'm not sure this method explains *everything* about how music organizes time. Still, the idea of a network of relations linking present, past and future through a system of expectation/frustration/fulfilment does seem a plausible approach to the way a lot of music works.

On the cassette I used the expression 'make sense'. And, though the exact nature of musical 'sense' is hard to be sure of, there is a widespread feeling that pieces either make sense or do not. So, without wanting to stretch an analogy with verbal language *too* far, I think there is some point to a comparison between the expectation-structure I've just been talking about and the structure of verbal syntax. There, too, each term in a unit (a sentence) is chosen from a finite set of options, the choice being governed by conventions – of grammar, vocabulary, style and context. In the following example, imagine I am speaking seriously to you, in private.

'I...'
[a wide range of words could follow]

'I love...'
[the options narrow – quite likely 'you', but could be 'Margaret Thatcher', 'drinking claret', or...]

'I love it...'
[relatively few options – 'here'?]

'I love it when you...'
[has to be an action – not many would be likely in the context]

'I love it when you smile'
[end. Or is it?]

'I love it when you smile at...'
[no – but it can now surely only be...]

'I love it when you smile at me'
[well, there could conceivably be some other objects of your smile; but this is the most likely – and anyway I'm a hopeful type]

The analogy with verbal syntax will be pursued further in Unit 9. Meanwhile, it's worth pointing out that it's a loose analogy. For one thing, language contains a much lower degree of immediate repetition than music does. For another, the factor of *meaning* is at once less central in music and more problematical – problematical because the levels of what in linguistics are called *denotation* (basic, unequivocal meanings of words) and *reference* (what these meanings relate to in the 'real world') seem to be absent. Still, I think there are enough similarities between verbal and musical syntax for the comparison to be useful.

4.2 GESTALT THEORY

The system I have just been describing isn't necessarily the only way musical time is organized; or to be more precise, it's not necessarily the only possible *explanation* for how musical organization of time makes sense. And it may be that other methods are sometimes more appropriate.

For example, it could be argued that the tune I made up on the cassette makes sense less through sampling each note as it comes, comparing it unconsciously against an inventory of possibilities, and more through a response to the shape of the tune as a whole. One way of following up this approach would be by drawing on *Gestalt theory*. This is a theory of perception developed by some German psychologists in the early twentieth century, and applied, then and since, quite widely within the fields of psychology, philosophy and the arts. The basic tenet is that the whole is greater than the parts; indeed, that the parts only make sense in relation to the whole, and that consequently we tend to *organize* our perceptions by *grouping* items into *patterns*. (Remember what I said about the tendency to group regular pulsations.) The *Gestalt* theorists formulated many 'laws' to explain how this worked. For our purposes, these boil down to the fundamental idea that perceivers' preferred shapes are always the *simplest* and most *stable*; this tends to imply a preference for symmetry, balance, regularity, smooth continuity and closure (i.e. a sense of completeness). Applied to tunes, this theory means that their pitch shape will often move smoothly; that the relationship of their parts will often seem to 'balance', to display symmetry; that directions of movement or patterns of rhythm will often continue in a predictable way; that the end will not leave us 'hanging in the air' but often come back to the same pitch as the beginning. If, for example, I tried to draw a 'picture' of the overall pitch-shape of my tune (associating an upward visual movement with an 'upward' movement in pitch: which, interestingly, is what people usually do), it would have a 'satisfying' arch structure, displaying symmetry, balance, smoothness and closure (Figure 1). Many tunes (though by no means all) do follow this pattern. Of course, this still leaves open the questions of *why* some shapes are satisfying, and of whether this

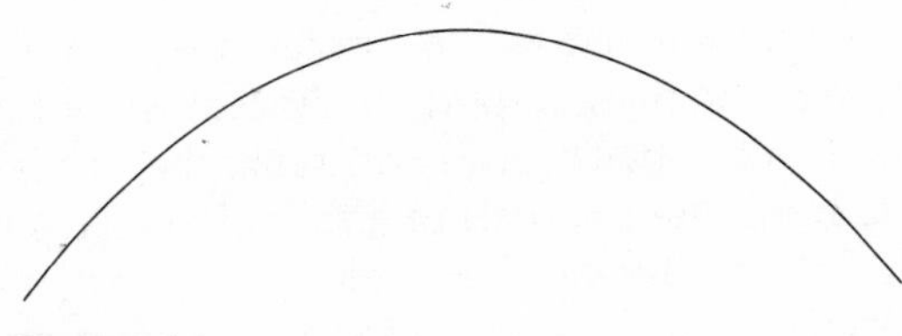

Figure 1

is a matter of innate brain function (as the *Gestalt* psychologists thought) or (as many psychologists now think more likely) a matter of cultural convention – which would bring us back to processes of learning and expectation. And it disregards the *context* in which the shape is satisfying. Maybe for some purposes a smooth arch shape would not be appropriate. Listeners may find it boring or bland; disturbance of *Gestalt* stability may in one sense be 'satisfying'. Or in some musical contexts an angular or asymmetric shape could be preferable for reasons of expression.

4.3 DEEP STRUCTURES AND SURFACE STRUCTURES

We could pursue a bit further the question of *overall* shape, and argue that this overall structure, far from being the pattern into which the parts are organized, exists on a different *level*, which is *relatively distinct* from those parts, from the details of what we actually hear. In other words, we would be making a distinction between a 'deep structure' – which we may well not be conscious of and which may be more or less hidden – and the explicit 'surface structure' which is actually sung or played. We could again draw on linguistics for this approach. The influential scholar Noam Chomsky and others argue that the reason language users can generate an infinite number of utterances, which they may never have heard before, is through their knowledge of 'deep structures' in the language *grammar*; the detailed permutations of vocabulary are simply fitted into the grammatical structures through the operation of various 'rules'. To give a very simple example, the grammatical structure 'subject-verb-object' could generate countless surface structures: 'I love you'; 'music uses sounds'; etc.

There's a not dissimilar approach in musical analysis, associated particularly with the early twentieth-century German theorist Heinrich Schenker, who suggested that in music 'deep structures' (he didn't call them that) were constituted by certain basic pitch relationships (for instance, the fifth, which I mentioned earlier).

Using either approach the implications would be that there could be lots of tunes, slightly different in detail (i.e. on the surface), sharing the same deep structure. And, according to this explanation, that shared deep structure would be the main reason for the fact that a specific tune 'makes sense'. Consider my little tune again (play cassette 3, side 1, band 3a). If you look at the diagram below, you can follow it by eye and ear simultaneously. You will have realised that the rhythm consists of an alternation of long and short notes; I represent these as a vertical stroke for a long note, a stroke with a tail for a short. And you will have realised that the tune falls into two units; these are marked by the horizontal square brackets.

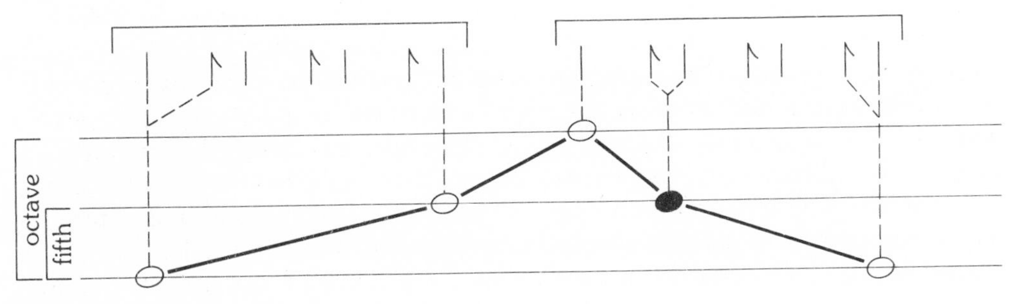

Figure 2

Most listeners will sense that the first and last notes of each unit (marked with a white oval) are structurally the most important. And these notes (together with a subsidiary note, marked with a black oval) constitute the primary intervals within the pitch system in use here: the intervals of fifth and octave which I mentioned earlier (see section 2). These intervals are 'spelled out' for you on the cassette (band 3b). These intervals could be seen as forming a deep structure, and the tune – the 'surface' – as simply an elaboration of this deep structure. Many other tunes could build a different surface on the same, or a similar, deep structure. For instance, 'Baa Baa Black Sheep' does so:

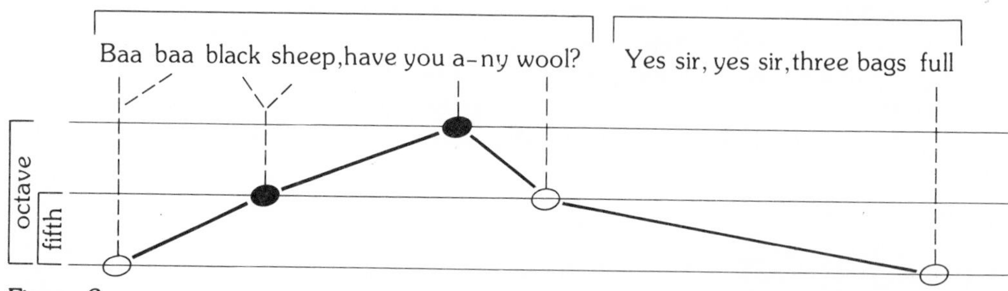

Figure 3

The first two phrases of 'Somewhere over the Rainbow' do too, though the deep structure is rather more hidden:

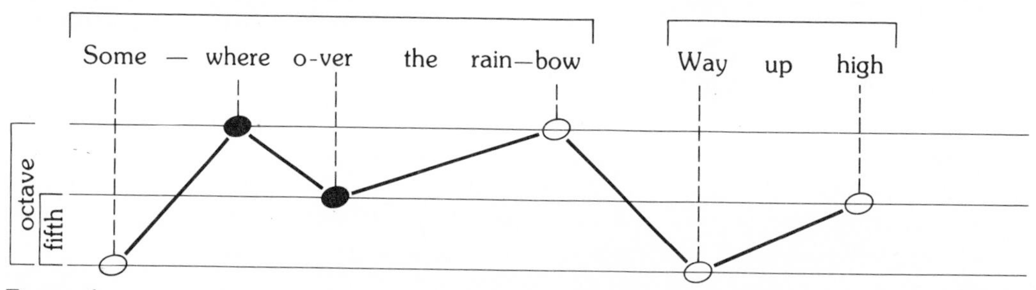

Figure 4

Gestalt analysis would see these three tunes as distinct: their pitch-shapes are quite different. Deep-structure analysis would see them as linked.

Again, the question then arises as to whether such deep structures are entirely conventional – that is, learned within particular cultures – or perhaps innate in human beings. In linguistics, too, this debate rages, with some arguing for a deep structure of the human mind which on a very basic level would link all languages, and others arguing that grammatical competence is a product of learning culturally-specific patterns. In music, Schenker saw his 'deep structural' pitch relationships as innate – as many theorists have. He himself accepted that any music not based on these relationships couldn't then, by definition, be 'good' music. As you will realize by now, I find this view hard to accept myself.

4.4 INTONATIONAL ANALYSIS

Turning back to the surface of the tune, a rather different way of using an analogy between musical and verbal utterances would be through a comparison of their respective rhythms and pitch-shapes (or *contours*). We could call this an *intonational* approach. (I am using the word 'intonational' as it applies to speech, rather than as it is used, in music theory, to refer to the tuning of notes.) I'm sure you will have noticed that when we speak, our utterances usually fall into units, marked off by breaths and pauses, that each of these units has an internal rhythm, and that each unit has a pitch-contour. A sequence of units may form a larger pitch-contour too. To give the simplest example, most statements fall in pitch towards the end; most questions rise. (At least, this is true of most British English use; I'm not sure how general it is.) Pitch-contours, rhythms and phrasings aren't just decorative; they contribute to meaning. So, one could see many tunes as mirroring the intonation of spoken utterances – or alternatively one could see both as products of a deeper principle of human behaviour or expression.

It's easy enough to find a spoken utterance which matches the pitch-contour and phrasing of my tune (underlining represents stress):

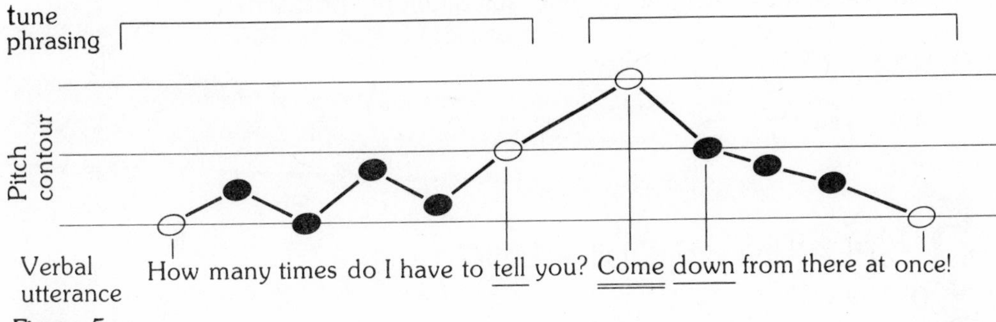

Figure 5

Of course, that tune doesn't *mean* those words; lots of other tunes and lots of other verbal utterances would fit the intonational patterns. Indeed, the tune doesn't exactly *mean* any words. So what's happening? Does the tune offer a kind of generalization, an abstraction, of a particular mode of human expressive behaviour, which spoken language also draws on but makes more concrete? I'm not sure. It's also obvious that the rise-and-fall shape is a very common one, in tunes and speech; the analogy doesn't always work for other shapes. But I do find this approach useful for a good deal of music; the close association of music and speech, in singing, isn't coincidental, I'm sure.

4.5 MOVEMENT

The rise-and-fall shape has analogies with *gestures* as well as speech. Out-and-back, up-and-down, in-and-out movements, and ways of mentally mapping the world, are deeply rooted. This brings us back to the physical sources of rhythm mentioned earlier (section 2). And we have rather neglected the rhythm of the tune. But obviously this will vitally affect the way the organization of time is felt – whether it marches, waltzes, jigs or whatever. Here again structures of expectation and of repetition and change will apply; and over and above that the rhythmic *style* will tend to produce important associations with kinds of movement and musical functions.

4.6 SUMMARY

This section could go on for a long time; there are many approaches to musical structure. But my aim isn't to be comprehensive – and there is no requirement, unless you're particularly interested, to remember all the details of all the methods outlined here. Rather, my purpose has been

1 to offer a few approaches to the organization of time in music which you may find useful and may try to apply later;

2 perhaps more importantly, to establish the point that all music is structured through 'rules': collectively accepted conventions, norms and styles. This isn't to deny the possibility of 'innovation' and 'creativity'; after all, the game of football is governed by rules and played in various styles, but rules and styles change, and neither enables us to predict in detail what a brilliant individual player might do. His innovations might even 'change the rules of the game'. Nor does the importance of conventions deny the possibility that there's a relationship between the systems of 'rules' and naturally occurring materials and capacities; football players have two feet, a head, etc., etc. What must be stressed, however, is that,

when all qualifications have been made, it is a particular music's system of 'rules' which is primary, since without it the music itself, as a way of 'making sense' to *groups* of people, couldn't exist.

3 I have also wanted to keep some openness about ways of understanding how the 'rules' work. Different individuals may find different approaches satisfying and useful; and different kinds of music may suit different approaches.

5 SPEAKING ABOUT MUSIC

Speaking about music is often regarded as a problem; at least this is true of 'academic' ways of speaking about music. People who make their living by doing it (like me) often seem to have a tendency to deny 'lay persons' (which probably – though not necessarily – includes you) the capability to do it properly. Conversely, lay persons often feel hesitant about trying to enter such a 'technical' area. But in the previous section we have been speaking about music quite readily: or to be more precise, *I* have been speaking – but I hope you have been following with not too much feeling of difficulty. Indeed, *everyone* speaks about music, even if it's only on the level of such statements as 'That's a lovely tune', 'The rhythm makes me want to dance', 'It sounds Spanish', 'That's not the right kind of music to have in church', 'The middle bit's so powerful', etc. Now those may seem rather *un*academic statements; but, if we regard music as in some sense a kind of language, they are examples of *metalinguistic* speech: that is, they are statements in one language (words) about another 'language' (music). And all speaking about music, of whatever kind, is first and foremost metalinguistic activity. To that extent the most forbidding music theory textbook gets no nearer to the music than the simplest descriptions of music's subjective effects.

During the course of the previous section, too, we discovered – unwittingly since this wasn't my primary focus – the two main avenues which speaking about music follows. We could label these the 'formalist' and the 'referentialist' approaches. The first wants to study music 'objectively', and regards its materials and processes as absolutely specific to music, and autonomous. The second, by contrast, holds that these materials and processes are linked with other areas of human experience, social structure or cultural practice; the links may be expressive (in which case the approach will be 'subjective') or they may be analogical, structural or causative: we saw some of the ways this might apply in the spheres of pitch relationships, rhythm and form, in the previous section. (Of course, the dispute between 'autonomy' and 'reference' isn't confined to music studies; it appears in all the arts disciplines, as you will remember from Unit 3.)

Exercise

The following statements all derive from discussion in the previous section. Can you allocate each to one of the two approaches, the 'formalist' (1) or the 'referentialist' (2)? Simply write the appropriate number against each statement.

1 Doing the same/doing something different are fundamental processes specific to music.

2 The meaning of tunes resides in their deep structure which reflects the laws of sound.

3 The musical principles of repetition and change are probably derived from wider patterns of experience.

4 All human experience is structured by rhythm, and this probably gives rise to musical rhythms.

5 Musical patterns make sense by drawing on conventions and structures of expectation which are uniquely musical.

6 Tunes are a form of musical 'speaking' and express meaning or feeling.

7 Various kinds of syntax, including musical syntax, all depend on making choices within a system governed by degrees of predictability.

8 Musical rhythms arise from and are specific to the nature of sound.

Suggested answer

Statements 1, 2, 5 and 8 are 'formalist'; statements 3, 4, 6 and 7 are 'referentialist'.

Further exercise

The statements fall into pairs, each pair constituting a formalist/referentialist opposition. Can you pair the statements?

Suggested answer

The pairs are 1 and 3; 2 and 6; 4 and 8; 5 and 7. If you got anything in this pair of exercises wrong, you should re-read section 4.

There has been considerable debate between the 'formalist' and 'referentialist' viewpoints, particularly within European musicology over the last two hundred years or so (musicology is the scientific study of music). Various other labels have been attached to the first viewpoint, as well as 'formalism' ('abstractionism' and 'objectivism' for example) and styles of music which are held to embody such tendencies disproportionately are often termed 'Classical' (a different sense of 'classical' from that which is more or less synonymous with 'serious', obviously). The second approach has given rise to such labels as 'expressionism' and 'subjectivism'; and styles which are thought of as particularly 'expressive', 'subjective' or 'referential' are often termed 'Romantic'. Both these tendencies go back a long way, certainly as far as classical Greece. In contrasting myths, a Homeric hymn tells how Hermes invented the lyre (the major string instrument of the time) when he realized that the shell of a turtle, if used as a sound-box, with strings attached, could produce sound; while Pindar describes how the art of playing the aulos (a primitive and raucous reed instrument, a bit like a double oboe) was invented by Athena when she heard the heartrending cries of Medusa's sisters after Perseus had killed the Gorgon. In the first, music arises as a result of an interest in producing sound, and in its properties; the lyre became associated with Apollo, and 'Apollonian' music with the 'inner harmony' of innate musical (and physical) laws. In the second myth, music arises as a response to subjective emotion; the aulos became associated with Dionysus and his orgiastic cults, and 'Dionysian' music with the expression of feeling and its overwhelming effects on listeners.

In more recent times, both tendencies have enjoyed periods of fashion. In the 'Romantic period' (quintessentially *c.* 1815–50, but to some extent the entire nineteenth century), 'expressionistic' and 'referentialist' views predominated. In the twentieth century, more 'scientific' and 'formalistic' ways of speaking about music have been prevalent. I'm not going to recommend either one to you, partly because this would be unfair, given that each side can claim many eminent theorists and critics in its support; partly because this is a decision which, if you take it, can be made only on the basis of a personal working through of methods; but mostly because my own, entirely personal view is that both tendencies are legitimate – or, to be more precise, that they're inextricably interconnected and, at the same time, may appropriately vary in proportions in accord with particular musics and purposes. Why are they 'inextricably interconnected'? Because each in a sense depends on the other. On the one hand, makers of music and listeners to music can, as social beings, only experience musical activity within socially defined circumstances; the musical structures don't work in a social vacuum, and at the very least, this implies an awareness of the *associations* of particular styles and performance contexts, and indeed an awareness of what music itself *is*, for that society. These are meanings which cannot just be read out of the music itself. At the same time, and on the other hand, extra-musical meanings and effects cannot come into being without the existence of those organized works which we call music; these works must make *internal* sense, that is, they function through an internally consistent system of conventions.

Given that this tension within ways of speaking about music exists – necessarily exists, in my view – it is nevertheless the case that, compared to the other arts, music does seem *more* self-absorbed, *more* self-referential. Words have an existence in everyday life; so do physical objects, shapes and colours. Words and physical phenomena give a way in to the analysis of literature and painting; there is here, on the whole, a level of reference to the 'real world' which is absent in music, where reference is much more 'internal' – from one theme to another, from a repetition to its precursor, from one note and the expectations it arouses to the next. I don't want to over-press this point, because it doesn't follow that words are used in the same way in literature (and shapes and colours in paintings) as in everyday life, or that there aren't systems of internal reference there too. Nevertheless, I think music does go significantly further in this respect, and so, just as literature and painting demand some specialized terms for their discussion – a metalanguage – so music requires a proportionately *more* specialized metalanguage. You can't describe patterns of musical sound without some special terms because nothing like these patterns exists outside of music. You can invent your own terms; we have seen that most people manage to speak about music through some metalanguage or other, though these are mostly not very precise about the internal musical organization. But it seems sensible to make use of a certain number of specialized terms established collectively over long periods by musicians; and it's one of the purposes of subsequent sections of this block to introduce you to some of them.

If speaking about music seems 'different', then, or even 'difficult' or 'technical', that's not because music is somehow 'mysterious', still less 'abstract', 'spiritual', 'intangible', or all the other airy adjectives used to justify the view that music is too precious to spend words on. It's simply because in everyday life sound (at least non-spoken sound) is less important, and less instrumental – that is, less involved in achieving practical ends – than words and physical objects. Music has always been regarded as more of a luxury practice, having to do with magic, play, ritual or the realm of the aesthetic as well as – perhaps more than – with 'practical' functions. The religious and ritual associations which surround music in so-called simple, primitive societies have been very slow to disperse; indeed, they have still not entirely done so, as those who have felt the 'bewitching' effects of a Wagner music drama or the 'Dionysian' involvement created at many rock concerts will testify. At the same time, the strongly *collective* nature of music making and listening has also been slow to disappear. The making, owning and enjoyment of books and paintings by individuals, in private, began long before similar developments in music. Even today, a high proportion of music making and listening is social activity. As a result, the pressure to communicate *about* music is at least as strong as the difficulties of doing so.

My main points in this section are simple ones. To summarize:

1 Speaking about music is inevitable; everybody does it.

2 Speaking about the extra-musical aspects of music – its emotional effects, the associations of style, analogies with other practices and experiences – is also inevitable; everybody does it, even musicologists, and it's not something to feel shamefaced about, as lots of lay persons do.

3 At the same time, to get very far in understanding music we need to attend to how those extra-musical aspects arise as a result of the shaping of *musical* structures. We need to speak about how the music itself is organized.

6 DOING ANALYSIS

In a sense, any act of speaking about music is an example of 'doing analysis'. Even if you just express enthusiasm for a tune, you're performing certain analytical operations: you're categorizing a certain experience as one that has arisen in response to something called 'a tune' – and we know that what a tune is, is very difficult to define precisely; it's certainly a matter of cultural convention, and thus you're drawing on your cultural experience and the ability you have acquired to sort sounds into 'tunes' on the one hand, 'not-tunes' (say, a random series of sounds) on the other. If the tune is accompanied, you're also separating the tune from the accompaniment; that is, you're distinguishing in your mind between different aspects of the overall musical *texture*.

So there's no rigid dividing line between 'speaking about music' and 'doing analysis'; there's a spectrum, and as you move from the first towards the second – which is what we want you to do in this block – all that happens is this:

1 your attention to the sounds and their effects becomes more concentrated, more focused;

2 the way that act of attention gives rise to responses (in words) becomes more self-aware – not a reflex but a considered mental process.

To start you off on this, I want you to listen to the four brief musical examples you first met in section 1 and to talk about them. They're bands 1a, b, c and d on the cassette.

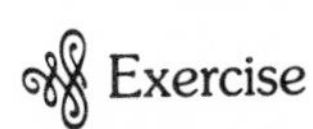

Exercise

Listen to the first example.
I think we will agree that what you hear comes within the category 'sound'. Are there any more precise statements we can agree about? You will remember thinking about the various aspects of sound – pitch, timbre, rhythm – in section 2. Listen again. Tell me which of these aspects seized your attention most.

Comments

There's very little sense of rhythm, because very little happens; for the first few seconds at least, the sound is static. There *is* a feeling of pitch – you can imagine that the sound could have been higher or it could have been lower – but again nothing much happens to it, certainly for the first few seconds. What hits you most, surely, is the sheer *quality* of the sound, its timbre.

Exercise

In fact, is there a *precise* pitch at all? Try to sing the pitch at the start of the example.

Comments

I suspect you found that hard. There *is* no single, precise, predominant pitch which one could sing along with. This is 'coloured noise' produced on a synthesizer. When *all* the frequencies within the audible frequency range are produced together in equal strength, the result is 'white noise'. When a particular band is selected out – all the frequencies between frequency X and frequency Y – the effect is known as 'coloured noise'.

Exercise

This doesn't mean that pitch is unimportant though, does it? Why not?

Comments

As we already saw, there is a sense of a pitch *level* or *area*. But also, after the first few seconds something happens to this level. It goes up, then comes back down; a *pitch contour* (an embryonic tune?) is created. It's simple to represent the effect visually:

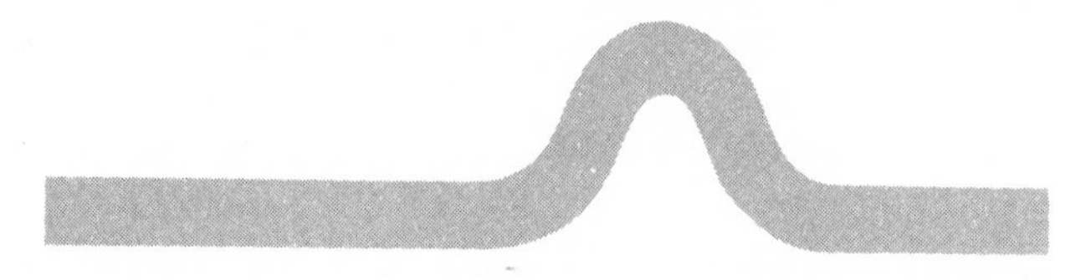

Figure 6

Whether you hear this as just sound or as 'music' depends very much on the context and on cultural conventions. You often get similar effects from your radio tuner; you would probably not think of them as music. But if this example was used in an electronic piece, it could easily result in 'musical' responses.

Exercise

Now listen to the second example. Do a similar exercise. That is, say which aspect(s) – pitch, rhythm, timbre – are important in producing the effect, and if you can, comment on how and why the particular aspects achieve this importance. Then say if any *other* aspect, beyond those three, impinges on your attention.

Comments

There is precise pitch. There are several singers and each one sings a precise note; indeed, each one keeps to the same note for considerable stretches of time.

Rhythm is also important. There's a pulse – or rather there are two, for the pulse changes part way through (where the predominant word changes from 'Vishnu' to something that sounds rather like 'why, why, why, what's day?'; it's not very clear, from the performance or the score, what these new words are supposed to be, but the extract does end with the 'answer' 'Monday'). And around these pulses there are various rhythmic patterns, often overlapping; the patterns are articulated in close conjunction with the words, which makes them easy to hear.

Timbre is straightforward -- human voices – and so perhaps less striking than in the previous extract. Nevertheless, the vocal quality is important in producing the particular effect; and there are things one could say about the way the voices are used.

Over and above all this, the pitches sung by the various singers coalesce into something else which adds a further dimension; we hear a *chord*, a *harmony*. You may not have been sure what word to use; but you probably felt the importance of what I'm describing. What is a chord? When several pitches sounded at the same time have the kind of relationships between themselves that result in the sensation of a recognized entity, a whole greater than the individual parts, we call that entity a chord. There's only one chord here; we hear the same combination of notes throughout the extract. 'Rich' and 'sensuous' are descriptive words that come to my mind for the chord, especially when it's heard complete in one insistent rhythm at the end of the extract. By no means all music uses chords, so the presence of this dimension is something to note. (There will be more discussion of harmony in Unit 8.)

The extract is taken, incidentally, from a much longer work (it lasts over an hour) called *Stimmung*, composed by the contemporary composer Karlheinz Stockhausen in 1968. The entire piece is a 'meditation' on this chord (no other notes are heard!), on particular sounds that can be made by this combination of voices, and on a set of 'magic names' (e.g. 'Vishnu', the name of a Hindu god).

 Exercise

Let's turn now to the third example. Just as in *Stimmung* the basic chord doesn't change, just as in our first, electronic, example the timbre doesn't change, so in this extract there are elements contributing to a distinctly static quality. Can you say what they are?

Comments

1 Rhythm. There's a basic rhythmic pattern, associated mostly with the drums, set up right at the start and unchanging throughout.

2 Harmony. As in *Stimmung*, there's only one chord throughout. (Listen to the guitar.)

You might also have commented on the tune. There are elements of repetition here, and you might feel that these contribute to a sense of a lack of change. However there are also elements of contrast.

 Exercise

Listen again, and try to describe how the use of repetition and contrast (doing the same/doing something different) works in the vocal parts. You will notice that there are two sections in the extract, which we can call 'verse' and 'refrain'.

 Comments

Both the 'verse' and the 'refrain' have a structure based on the same principle: alternation. In the verse (the first, narrative section), the lead vocalist sings just one phrase, repeated several times (it is *slightly* different sometimes, but the basic shape is always the same). This alternates with a different phrase, again repeated over and over, sung by the backing singers. The refrain ('Hey, Bo Diddley') is similar – phrase 1 (lead), phrase 2 (backing), phrase 1, phrase 2, and so on – but here the two phrases are more or less the same in shape.

Two very common principles of musical organization are involved here: if you like, two very common ways of organizing the relationship of repetition and contrast. When a phrase is repeated over and over, it's called an *ostinato*, or alternatively – by Afro-American and popular musicians – a *riff*. When one phrase or performer alternates with another, this is called *antiphony*, or alternatively – in the African and Afro-American traditions – it's known as *call and response*. As you can hear, both are used here. When they are combined, various permutations can appear; two are employed in this song.

For those who don't recognize the extract, it comes from a recording by the black American rhythm 'n' blues singer, Bo Diddley, called 'Hey Bo Diddley', made in 1955.

That third example, compared to the first two, lays much more stress on *tune structure*: things happen as we move along and those things divide up the song into units. That tendency is even stronger in our last example, which is an unaccompanied tune; and I would like you to concentrate wholly on the tune structure.

 Exercise

Can you answer these questions:

1 How many units (phrases) does the tune divide into?

2 Do these phrases repeat each other musically, or are they all different, or do their relationships fall into some other pattern?

To get you off on the right track, I'll identify the first phrase. It goes to the words 'Amazing grace, how sweet the sound'.

Comments

1 Four. They follow the structure of the words, as follows:

Phrase 1 Amazing grace, how sweet the sound

Phrase 2 That saved a wretch like me.

Phrase 3 I once was lost but now I'm found

Phrase 4 Was blind but now I see.

2 The first thing to do is to make a distinction between *essential notes* and *ornamental notes.* Essential notes constitute the 'bones' of the tune; by and large they come *on* the beat and initiate syllables. Between some of them the singer adds decorative notes. Considering only the essential notes, we find that the same basic rhythmic pattern continues almost unceasingly throughout the tune. It's an alternation of long note and short note (in a ratio of 2/1). So that's an element of repetition. What about pitch-contour? We need to listen to this quite carefully – and it will be helpful to look too, so I'll use some of the graphic representations introduced in section 4. My diagrams include only the essential notes. notes.

The easiest place to start is with phrases 2 and 4, which you will find are musically almost identical; only the final note is different: in phrase 2 it goes up, giving an 'unfinished' effect, while in phrase 4 it falls, in such a way that it signifies a 'closure'. (Such phrase-endings are called *cadences,* by the way; this is true of speech – especially poetics and rhetoric – as well as music. Cadences are either 'open' – 'unfinished' – or 'closed'.)

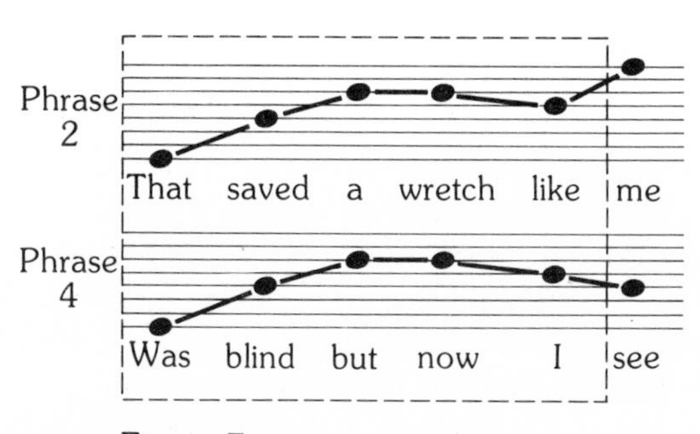

Figure 7

Sing the tune to yourself, or play the recording again, and check the phrase shapes against my diagram.

Now sing, or listen to, phrases 1 and 3. Can you hear that, again, they're almost the same as each other? In this case the *beginnings* are slightly different, but otherwise they're identical.

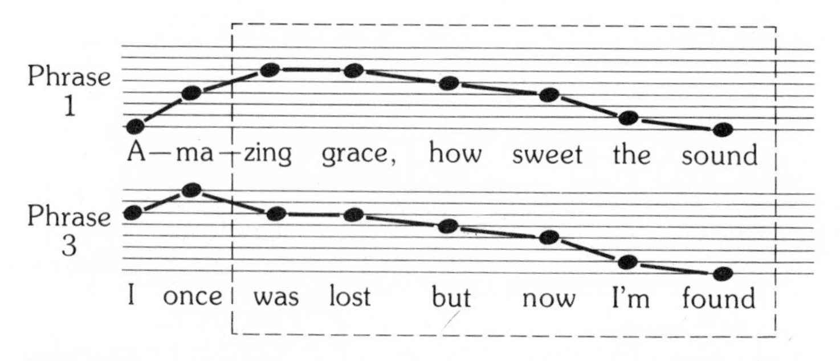

Figure 8

It looks, then, as if we have this kind of structure: ABAB. But on further listening it becomes clear that A isn't *that* different from B: the beginnings *and* endings are varied, but the middle is still the same; and three out of the four phrases have a very high degree of identity (see Figure 9).

Again, you might find it helpful to play the recording once more and follow it phrase by phrase on the diagram.

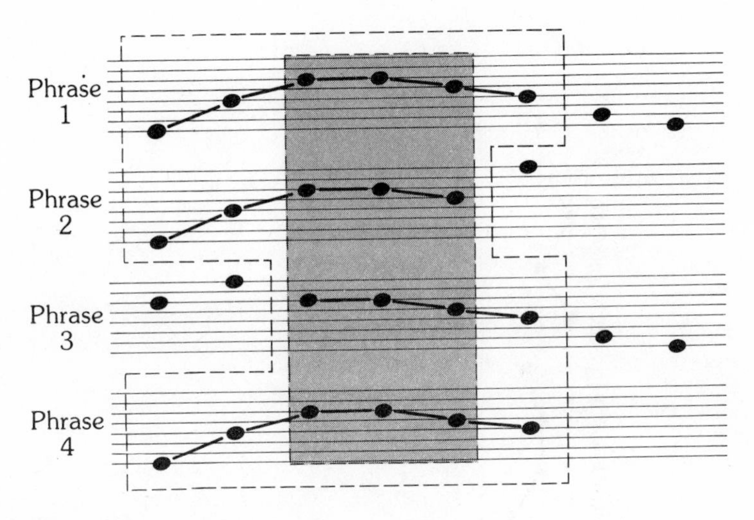

Figure 9

So in one sense the tune is all repetition (every phrase basically the same), but in another it's all contrast (every phrase slightly varied). You could regard the result as very simple – or very subtle; I think it's both – certainly a lot of tunes, from many cultures, adopt this variants-on-repeated-framework technique. To some extent, whether you emphasize the degree of repetition or the degree of variation will depend on which analytical approach you use. For instance, an emphasis on 'deep structure' would produce a focus on what the phrases have in common. By contrast, a stress on overall pitch contour (the tune *Gestalt*) would note the rise in pitch in the middle of the tune (end of phrase 2/beginning of phrase 3) which compared to the pitch level at the beginning and end, produces a central arch-like peak in the overall wave shape of the tune; the result is a distinct degree of symmetry. In this approach, the phrase variants would be seen as important, for they shape the tune into an *entity* (see Figure 10 overleaf).

You may well be familiar with this tune. Even if you don't know the hymn, you may have heard the tune, to different words, at football matches or on TV's 'Match of the Day'. Interestingly, football crowds tend to substitute phrase 2 for phrase 4, and then repeat phrases 2 and 3 *ad infinitum* (try it to 'Ipswich' or 'Arsenal' or whatever). By that simple change, an increased emphasis on the tune's repetitive qualities is produced, for the final note one expects (the 'closure' effected by the last note of phrase 4) never comes and the singing can go on 'for ever' (see Figure 11 overleaf).

In terms of information theory, one's expectations for that final note aren't fulfilled, which can be frustrating – until one realizes that the tune's meaning and function have changed, and with them the musical conventions. A self-sufficient hymn with a lyric completeness, expressing 'symmetrical' sentiments ('grace' ⟷ 'wretch'; 'lost' ⟷ 'found'; 'blind' ⟷ 'see'), has changed into a collective chant which can circle round endlessly, expressing continuing support for the team. This is a good illustration, I think, of the links between internal musical system and external social context which I stressed earlier.

The next unit in this block focuses on the internal musical system. We have already begun to discover something about the basic aspects of music – pitch, rhythm, timbre, and so on. The next unit looks at these in more detail.

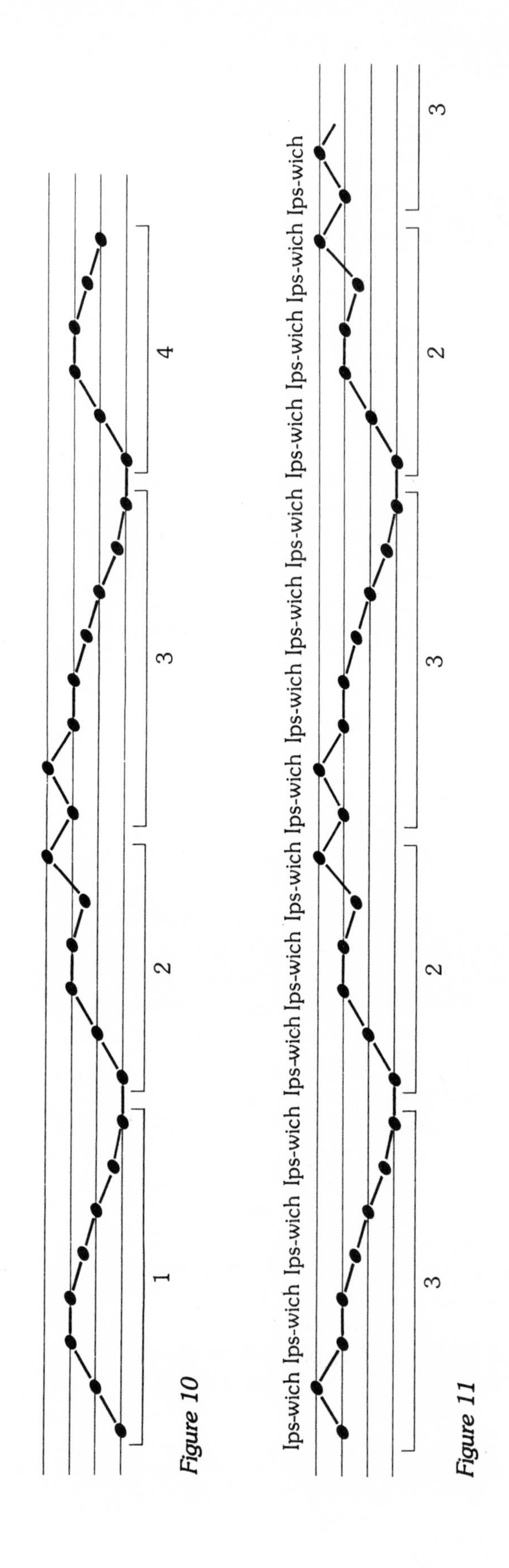

Figure 10

Figure 11

Unit 8

Contributors

Bill Strang has written Part I on the basis of an idea originally developed by the late Dinah Barsham; Donald J. Burrows has written Part II.

PART I LISTENING TO THE ELEMENTS OF MUSIC

1 INTRODUCTION

The next section of this *Introduction to Music* is based on material you will find on cassette 3. Read this introductory section carefully before turning to the cassette. Then work through side 1, band 4 'Listening to the Elements of Music' and the exercise which follows at the beginning of side 2 as band 1. You will need to keep this unit to hand as you listen, so that you can refer to the notes printed below.

It is important that you should listen to the cassette at this stage because the material in Unit 8 Part II and Unit 9 assumes you have grasped its content; so please resist the temptation to skip the cassette or leave it till later: it is as important a part of this introduction to music as the written sections.

Take a counter-reading at the start of band 4, as you may want to listen to it more than once. In the course of the cassette I will ask you to look at the following notes. They contain definitions of several basic musical terms and diagrams illustrating some of these, using pieces you will hear on the cassette. The notes also serve as a summary of my discussion which you may find helpful for revision.

Details of the performances of all the extracts played on the cassette can be found in the Cassette Notes.

Turn on cassette 3, side 1, band 4, now.

1st Piece. COUNTER READING 100
2nd Piece " " 148

2 NOTES TO ACCOMPANY THE CASSETTE TALK

Note 1 *Rhythm*: the aspect of music concerned with the distribution of sounds in time.

Note 2 Rhythm includes three more basic elements:

Duration: the length of a sound in time, or how long it lasts

Beat: a regular pulse

Metre: the grouping of accented and unaccented beats which serves as a skeleton or framework for the rhythm

Grouping in twos (as in a March):

Grouping in threes (as in a Waltz):

A rhythm is a succession of similar or varying durations set against the regular background or framework of the metre.

Note 3 Rhythm from the beginning of Ravel's *Bolero*:

Metre (regular framework)

Rhythm

Alternative way of showing rhythm

Note 4 *Melody*: a series of notes which have different pitches, or occasionally the same pitch; what most people would call 'the tune'

Pitch: how high or low a note is

Note 5 Pitch-contour of plainsong melody

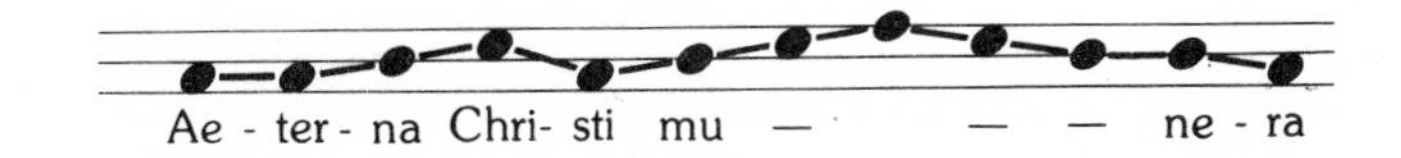

This melody moves mainly by steps.

Note 6

Didn't we have a lovely time the day we went to Bangor,

A beautiful day, we had lunch on the way, and all for

under a pound you know,

But on the way back I cuddled with Jack and we opened a bottle of cider,

Singin' a few of our favourite songs as the wheels went round.

Code: represents a large leap in the tune

Note 7 *Chord*: several notes sounding simultaneously

Harmony: can mean the same as 'chord'. But it is more often used to refer to successions of chords and the relationships between them.

Note 8 The first phrase of 'Abide with Me'

The top line of notes comprises the tune. The phrase can also be read as a series of chords. Each box contains a chord.

Note 9 *Counterpoint*: the simultaneous combination of two or more melodies (adjective: contrapuntal)

Note 10 Diagram of a round or canon: 'London's Burning'

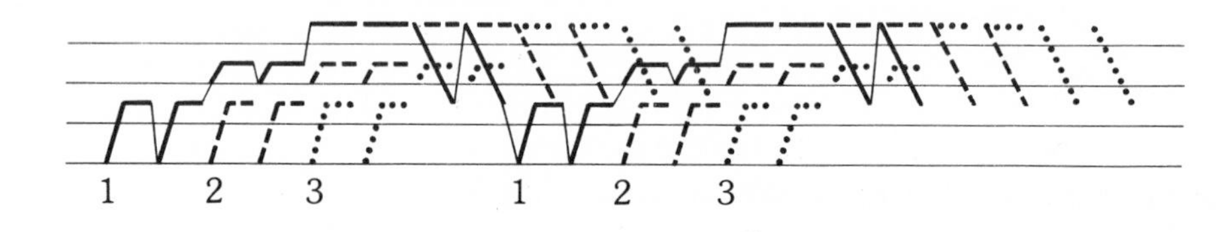

Note 11 Diagram of contrapuntal music:
Kyrie I from Palestrina: *Missa Aeterna Christi Munera*

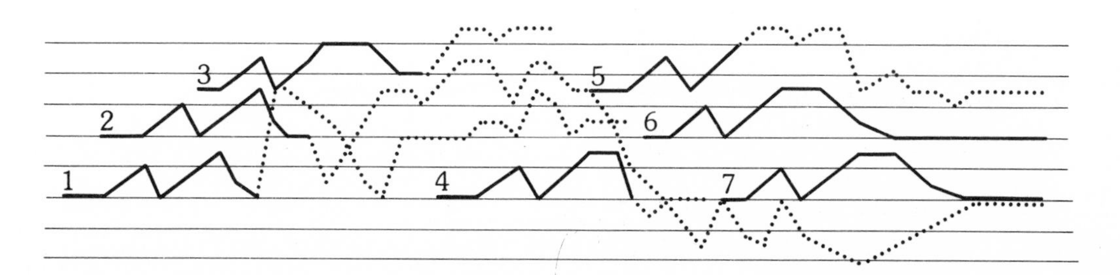

Note 12 *Texture* in ordinary speech, anything woven, a web. Used in music to indicate whether a piece is organized as a succession of chords (harmonic texture) or as a combination of several lines (contrapuntal texture)

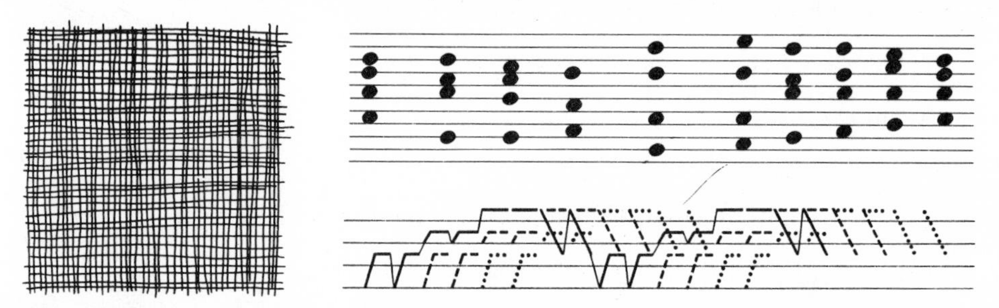

The threads that are stretched out lengthwise in a loom are called the warp: those that are woven into and across them the weft or woof.

A harmonic texture (top) is one which stresses the chordal aspect of the music. A contrapuntal texture (below) stresses the linear aspect.

Note 13 Texture is also used more loosely, e.g. to distinguish simple and complex textures, light and heavy, thick and thin.

Note 14 *Timbre* or *tone-colour*: the quality which distinguishes a note on one instrument or voice from the same note performed on other instruments or voices

Note 15 The sections (or families) of the standard symphony orchestra and the instruments usually found in each section.

Woodwind section – flutes, oboes, clarinets, bassoons

Brass section – horns, trumpets, trombones, tuba

String section – violins, violas, cellos, double basses

Percussion section – timpani (also called kettledrums): these are tuned to a definite pitch which can be varied. Side drum, bass drum, cymbals: these are of indefinite pitch.

Note 16 *Dynamics*: the gradations of loudness and softness in music

3 NOTES TO ACCOMPANY THE EXERCISE (CASSETTE 3, SIDE 2, BAND 1)

Turn first to the cassette where the exercise is introduced.

3.1 HOW TO APPROACH THE EXTRACTS

Take the extracts one at a time.

Take a counter-reading and listen to each extract at least twice.

Jot down which elements strike you as most obvious: try to say why. How are they operating?

Check the other elements: are they contributing anything significant?

Read the discussion in the unit.

Listen to the extract again at least once.

3.2 DISCUSSION OF THE EXTRACTS

Extract 1 Michael Tippett: Symphony No. 2, opening

I think there are three main elements to note in this extract. The first is the rhythm given out by the lower strings at the very beginning. Before this has finished, the second element, a horn-call, begins: this has a smooth melody in longer notes but you may have been more aware simply of the warm penetrating colour or timbre of the horns. The third element is another melody, albeit a rather jagged one, played by the high strings – the violins: this begins after about eight seconds. So there are three contrasting layers laid one on top of the other, as it were, to make a complex but lively musical texture. Each layer focuses on a different element. I would say that these are the most important aspects of this extract.

However, you may also have commented on the harmony; you may have felt it was rather dissonant. When the horns enter they don't seem to fit with what the lower strings are doing — the harmony is quite gritty. The dynamic is obviously loud: an appropriately positive beginning to a large-scale piece. Indeed, you could say that all the elements I have identified are very vigorous and the combination very quickly sets up many possibilities for energetic, even explosive interplay.

Return to the cassette now and play the extract again. After it you will find a few further words of advice to listen to before tackling the rest of the exercise.

Extract 2 Mozart: Clarinet Concerto, second movement

I think melody and timbre are the most important elements in this extract. It starts with a slow tune for the clarinet, gently accompanied by the string section of the orchestra, which provides the harmony. The whole orchestra repeats this tune at a louder dynamic level. When the clarinet re-enters, Mozart gives it a tune calculated to exploit the warm beauty of its tone quality. As an additional detail you may have noticed that the strings share this tune, entering into a little dialogue with the clarinet.

Extract 3 Queen: Bohemian Rhapsody

This extract falls into two sections, in effect the first two verses of a song. But perhaps the most striking elements in the first section are not the melody but the harmony and the timbre of the voices: these are very closely linked and work together to create interesting and subtly changing colours. Initially the voices all move together but later they have some independence, dividing temporarily into tune and accompaniment or backing. When the piano enters about halfway through this section it uses the same chords as the voices but breaks them up, introducing a new texture. In the interlude between the two sections the piano settles into a more regular pattern which is then maintained as an accompaniment to the solo voice. It is obviously this melody that predominates in the second half but from the words 'throw it all away' and the cymbal roll the bass is given greater prominence and the rhythm is underlined more emphatically. But overall I would say that the most interesting elements of this extract are its constantly changing texture and timbre.

Extract 4 Beethoven: Symphony No. 7, second movement

The most important element here is the rhythm. The pattern — – – — — (long, short short, long, long) is repeated four times for each phrase, the only deviation being the silence at the end of each phrase. In the first half there is minimal melodic interest – stepwise movement within a very narrow range. In fact you may have been equally aware of the chordal texture. You may also have noted the change in dynamic (quieter) or commented on the low close texture or sombre colour (low stringed instruments – no violins). None of these elements is allowed any room to expand and as a result the serious, rather claustrophobic atmosphere is intensified. The second half repeats the first, the main change being the addition of a more flowing melody in the middle of the texture. This creates a more linear or contrapuntal effect. It also raises the question of what the opening half has been – was it just the accompaniment perhaps? The plan resembles the opening of Ravel's *Bolero* which you heard during the talk, only here the opening rhythmic pattern has been greatly extended.

Extract 5 Holst: Mars, the Bringer of War

There are two main elements in this extract. Most obviously and consistently there is a strong rhythm which is repeated throughout: sometimes it is very prominent and at other times it becomes almost submerged, but it is always present. Then there is a melody that gradually emerges from fragmented, groping gestures at the beginning. Dynamics are also important: the volume increases from a fairly loud robust opening to a louder climax at the end of the section played.

These are the main points, but you might also have noticed the prominence of the brass section of the orchestra in the emerging tune, which contains some fanfare-like gestures, and the percussion, which emphasizes the rhythm at times – so timbre also plays a significant part.

In view of the title it is reasonable to observe that all these technical factors contribute to the impression of the approach of some war-like threat. This sort of comment would have been less appropriate to the Tippett example, despite some similarities, since Tippett gives no indication that he has any descriptive idea in mind.

One final and subtle point about *Mars*: you may have noticed that the melody is sometimes expressed as chords, especially at the point where it emerges into the fanfare gestures – so there is a harmonic element too.

If you got the main three points – rhythm, emerging tune and increasing dynamic – well done. If you didn't, listen to the extract again and see if you can hear them now. If you did, it would still be a good idea to round off your work on this extract by listening again: perhaps this time you will also be able to savour the more subtle points I have mentioned.

Extract 6 Sondheim: Send in the Clowns

This is a song, so melody is obviously an important element. The tune moves very slowly. It is broken into short phrases and sung in a dry voice that sounds almost as if it has cracked deeper down. The accompaniment provides an unbroken cushion of harmony: the chords also change very slowly. The timbre of this accompaniment is very striking – gentle, warm string tone flecked with the plucked string tone of the harp. The tune is anticipated by the clarinet introduction, whose rich warm timbre also contrasts with the dry tone of the voice. In between the phrases of the tune wisps of melody emerge from other instruments – these are always gentle and lyrical. So it seems that every other aspect of this piece is designed to act as a foil to the melody and the particular timbre of the singer's voice.

Extract 7 Handel: Zadok the Priest, opening section

I think the element of greatest importance here is harmony. The same chord is repeated several times, usually eight times, before changing, usually on a strong beat. The effect is of a slow-moving harmony which has been decorated with repetitions. This decoration is taken further by the addition of a rising figure in the violins which spells out the chord a note at a time as a linear/melodic gesture (like singing doh-me-soh-doh, if you know sol-fa): this is also repeated. You may have been more immediately aware of the melodic quality of the rising violin figure or the rhythmic repetition of the chords but I put the harmony first because all these other elements are eventually gathered up into it. So the texture is made up from repeated chords with a more elaborate repeated pattern superimposed on top. Dynamics are also important in that there is an increase, gradual at first, up to the very loud and dramatic choral entry. The choir has a bold chordal texture, behind which the orchestra maintains the same decorative figuration as before.

This is the beginning of a piece written for the coronation of King George II and Queen Caroline. Hence the choice of text with its reference to the anointing of the Old Testament King, Solomon. Handel combines a dignified processional feeling (slow-moving chords) with an impression of rich decoration (the chords are encrusted, as it were, with the rising string figures), two qualities that would doubtless have characterized the splendid circumstances of its first performance. Loud choral shouts of acclamation would also have been appropriate to the occasion; at the climax of the piece the choir actually sings 'God save the King' in repeated exclamations. Thus the technical musical means employed reflect the occasion for which the music was conceived. This is an aspect of music we have barely touched on yet, so you may not have made that connection: Donald Burrows will take up the theme of the relationship between the composer, the music and the audience later, in Unit 9.

PART II SYNTAX AND STRUCTURE: ELEMENTS BECOME LANGUAGE

1 INTRODUCTION

You could describe the act of musical composition as the art of putting together the elements that you encountered in Part I. As the title to this section implies, I want to suggest some parallels between music and verbal language as a useful way of coming to grips with the nature of composition. Richard Middleton has already introduced you to this idea in Unit 7, section 4, where he gave several examples of useful parallels between the two. Students often go rather blurry-eyed as soon as musical composition is mentioned, and seem to think that the whole process is a mysterious one of 'inspiration', beyond their reach or understanding. To some extent the process *is* rather mysterious, but there is also much about it that is accessible and I hope that the parallels with language will help you to retrace part of the process of a composer's work without too much difficulty. I am aware of the fact that, although we all use verbal communication every day, very few people have reason to stop and think about their habitual use of language, and fewer still would have the patience to analyse it in any detail. It is indeed often a surprise to find that you have been speaking prose all your life, and using nouns, verbs and conditional clauses without realising it. Yet language 'works' nevertheless, just as music 'works'. I do not intend to go into any great technicalities about either language or music in this section, but I hope that the occasional cross-references will help you to relate musical ideas, techniques and structures to verbal ones with which you are already familiar.

Let us begin by sampling some verbal structures. Consider these sentences:

1 R:srneiehg érniecr̊ to efr ceptg icctnhiegtgtc ntg@jured.

2 Pace thought in previous the works own.

3 They sees the men.

4 The soul is green.

5 The book is on the table.

I have arranged them in an order from the least comprehensible to the most straightforward. The first sentence consists virtually entirely of nonsense words, the second contains accepted words but randomly arranged, the third makes more 'sense', but the syntax is defective – that is, the words 'they sees' do not agree because the first is plural and the second is singular. We might nevertheless understand the meaning of the third sentence, making allowance for this. The fourth sentence is grammatically correct, but involves terms that present some difficulty – what is a soul? How would a person who was red/green colourblind understand it? Only the last sentence of the five is sufficiently problem-free to lead to the assumption that most people would understand the same thing from it. We could all agree that it 'made sense'.

Music relies on some form of coherence and a composer is someone who, in addition to having good musical ideas as such, has to develop coherent ways of fitting them together. I would like you to notice that I said *some form* of coherence. In some dialects, sentence 3 might be a perfectly acceptable usage: a poet might be able to make something of sentences 1–3 and might even reject sentence 5 as being too direct, too prosaic. A communication problem arises if a poet's attempt to explore 'deeper' levels of meaning through an unconventional use of language is written off by his listeners as nonsense. There are different forms and modes of coherence, in music as in language, and experimentation with new forms of coherence is a feature of the work of many twentieth-century composers.

The nineteenth-century musical examples that will be used in this section rely on systems of coherence that you should find fairly easy to grasp. For most people who have grown up within 'European' cultures, the nineteenth-century musical style remains the basis of their conventional appreciation of music whether they realize it or not. Often it is the style they prefer to listen to, and it has a large influence on the commercial music being written today. It is still our musical equivalent of sentences 4 and 5.

In this section I shall not attempt to give equal attention to all of the musical elements that were identified in Part I. I want us to concentrate on short pieces of music for piano in which timbre and texture remain fairly constant, so that we can follow through the process by which the composer builds up rhythmic and melodic elements into a piece of music. In order to deal with rhythm and melody effectively, I have not avoided the use of simple musical notation. This may not look very accessible at first, but I am sure that you will surprise yourself with the success that you can achieve if you follow the exercises carefully. Bear in mind that, for our purpose, *the written music is simply a way of recording visually the sounds that you hear.*

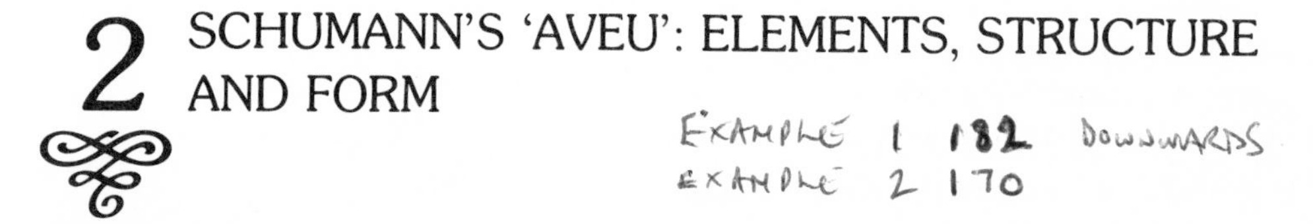

2 SCHUMANN'S 'AVEU': ELEMENTS, STRUCTURE AND FORM

2.1 MAINLY RHYTHM

'Aveu' comes from *Carnaval*, a set of piano pieces composed by Robert Schumann (1810–56) in 1834–5: I shall give you a little of the background to the composition later on when we deal with melodic elements. The texture is a simple one of tune-and-accompaniment. The tune is the uppermost part throughout. Beneath the tune there is a regularly-moving accompaniment, but you can ignore this for the moment, as we are going to concentrate on the tune.

Introductory listening

First of all, simply play the piece through to familiarize yourself with the sound and the length. (Perhaps I should say 'brevity' rather than length – it is the shortest piece in *Carnaval*). The tape examples for this section are on cassette 3, side 2, band 2. Each example is announced in turn. Example 1 is the complete piece: please find that now and make a note of the current counter reading, because you will be returning to play the piece through several times.

Now play example 1 (the complete piece) through twice.

The piece comprises two sections: a short section (repeated) followed by a slightly longer one (also repeated). Immediately after example 1, to which you have just listened, you will find the complete piece given again, but with the sections broken up (example 2). Again, take a counter reading, as you may find this presentation helpful later on.

Now play example 2 through twice, and try to recognize where the musical divisions between sections come. You can test yourself by going back to example 1 and trying to spot the sections without my help!

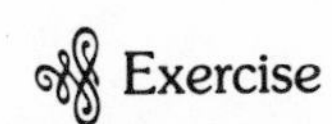 Exercise

We shall now concentrate on the rhythm of the opening phrase. As example 3 on your tape you will find the opening phrase of the tune played without the accompaniment. Here is its rhythm:

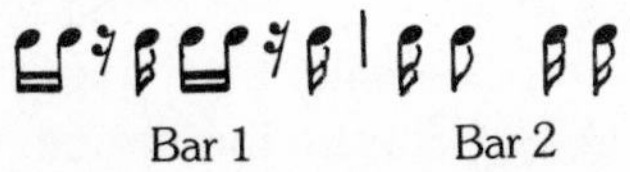

Bar 1 Bar 2

Figure 1

Now find example 3 on your tape. (Please take a counter reading, as you will use this example again later.) The phrase is played four times. I suggest that for at least one playing you try putting your finger on the notes given above as they are played*. It is also a good idea to try clapping the rhythm. Repeat example 3 as often as you find useful. When you think that you are thoroughly familiar with this phrase, go on to the next exercise.

Listening to the rhythm in context

Now go on to example 4 on the tape and listen to the tune of the first phrase with its accompaniment. It is played twice.

Exercise

You will be using example 5 several times, so please take a counter reading now. Example 5 gives you the complete first section, with the repeats. It is played first 'melody only' and then with accompaniment.

The first section consists of two phrases: the one you heard in examples 3 and 4, followed by a new one.

Play example 5. What do you notice about the rhythm of the phrase that immediately follows the first one?

(Remember – you have two chances to hear this at each playing because the first section, consisting of the two phrases I want you to compare, is repeated.)

Answer

The second phrase repeats the rhythm of the first.

There is one 'linking note' between the two phrases, and this may have caught you out slightly, but I expect that most of you spotted the repetition. If you did not (or even if you did), I would like you to play the first section again and listen carefully to this feature. Here is the rhythm of the complete first section: again, I recommend that you try following the notes and clapping the rhythm as well as simply listening.

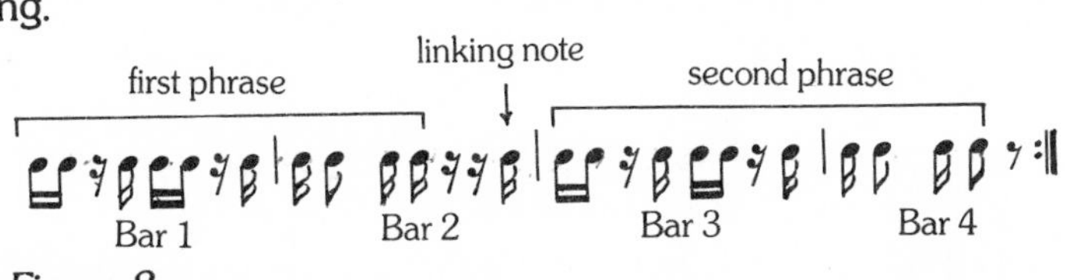

Figure 2

The sign :‖ indicates that the section is repeated. Sometimes, for clarity, the section to be repeated is shown within repeat-marks, thus ‖: :‖

Now play example 5 again, several times if possible, following the rhythm. You may have noticed from the musical notation that the final notes of the two phrases are not written as exactly the same lengths – but you would need very sharp ears to notice this, even from an exactly literal performance.

**When I ask you to 'follow the music' I suggest that you follow the 'blobs' or note heads. Each one of these denotes a sound. The sign 𝄾 marks a brief rest or silence. The vertical line is a 'bar line' and does not itself represent a sound. Bar lines mark regular metrical units within the rhythm, and I have included them in your musical examples because they provide useful visual landmarks.*

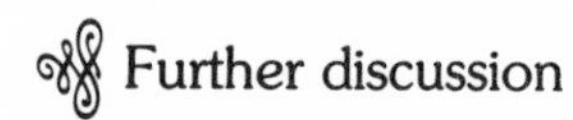

Further discussion

Richard Middleton referred in Unit 7 to the repetition/contrast balance as a fundamental feature of musical composition. Obviously, repetition is an important resource for a composer. But you might say to yourself: 'The same rhythm twice, and then repeated – four times in all: isn't that going to be rather boring?' My answer would be 'Well, that is a possibility, but it partly depends on how well written the basic element is'. In fact Schumann's rhythm has a rather satisfying shape. The first two notes are not very interesting in themselves, except perhaps in their brevity, for we cannot believe that this tiny fragment by itself constitutes a tune! Rather, these two notes function like a single word starting a sentence. The whole phrase broadens out from this opening, thus:

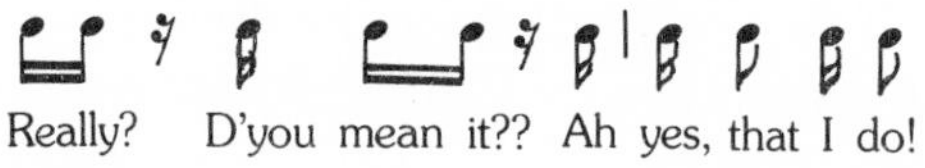

Really? D'you mean it?? Ah yes, that I do!

Figure 3

2.2 MELODY

Still concentrating on the two phrases that make up the first section of 'Aveu', let us now look at the melody. In a sense there is little new to add here, because the melody reinforces the pattern I have just outlined – it is designed to 'mean' the same thing as the rhythm. I will represent the three elements of the opening phrase by the signs ? – ?? – ! Here is the melody of the first phrase. Again, don't be put off by the musical notation if you are not familiar with it: in fact, most people find it easier to recognize the rise and fall of a melody on the lines and spaces of a conventional musical stave than to follow a rhythm.

Figure 4

Exercise

Wind the tape back to example 3 and listen to the opening again (as many times as you need), following this music example. Once more, I recommend that on at least one playing you follow the music with your finger. Try especially this time, as we are concentrating on the melody, to put your finger near to the *heads* (i.e. the 'blobs') of the notes, because these mark the pitch.

Now, can you suggest how the melody reinforces the ? – ?? – ! pattern?

Answer

The pitch levels of the notes follow the pattern suggested by the rhythm. More specifically:

? is characterized by the *rising* pitch of the first two notes, then

?? stays around the same pitch, as if waiting for developments. It's almost like trying to get a car to start!

! Ah! the melody achieves lift-off (or, if you prefer, the engine fires at last!) with a big leap upwards and, having achieved motion, can afford to fall back a little, releasing the tension at the end.

The whole melody, therefore, looks like this:

Figure 5

If I now extract the line that I have drawn through the noteheads marking the pitch levels, the pattern will be clear:

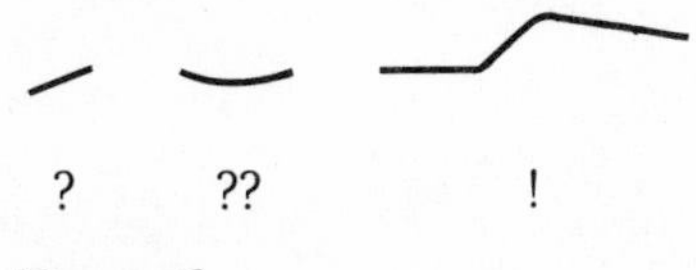

Figure 6

You will realize, I am sure, that these lines are 'pitch contours' of the type that you met in Unit 7, section 4.4.

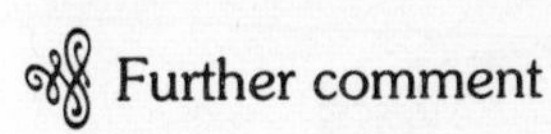

Further comment

We have perhaps rather laboured a mere two bars, but you have to remember that this is a very short piece, and in terms of the total length these two bars are, if anything, rather a long time. I suppose that it is in the creation of thematic material that some element of 'inspiration' is part of the composition process, but even in these two bars, a lot of thought has gone into the construction of the theme. For every tune that 'drops from heaven', there are many more that have to be evolved, and the first idea that occurs to a composer is not always the best. Beethoven kept sketch-books which are covered with experiments for themes: even some of his most natural-sounding tunes are the result of a lot of 'art'. The impetus (we might almost call it the 'story') behind Schumann's tune is rather curious. Schumann dedicated *Carnaval* to Ernestine von Fricken, a young pianist with whom he had a brief and none-too-serious affair. Ernestine was born in Asch in Bohemia. As you probably know, we use alphabetical letters to denote musical pitches: in the English-speaking world the letters A to G are used, but a slightly different system applies in German-speaking countries. It so happens that the possible 'musical' letters from Schumann's name, using the German system, were SCHA, an anagram of Asch. Schumann begins the melodies of many of the pieces in *Carnaval* with the musical notes that he called AsCH or SCHA. 'Aveu' is one of these, for it begins with the notes A flat-C-B(natural), equivalent in German alphabetical notation to As-c-h:

Figure 7

As an inspiration, this was perhaps rather trivial: the point really is that it started Schumann on various chains of thought, of which 'Aveu' was one of the results. The title 'Aveu' itself means 'Avowal' (an assertion or promise), but apart from the 'Passionato' direction to the performer (presumably reflecting the strength of the promise) I do not think that we need attach too much importance to the title. Also, I had better point out that most composers do not use an alphabetical stimulant when inventing themes! Back to the music!

2.3 PITCH-STRUCTURE OF THE MELODY

Let us now look beyond the first two bars. We noticed that bars 3–4 had the same rhythm as bars 1–2. What about the melody?

Exercise

Find example 5 on the tape and play it again. Does the second phrase (bars 3–4) follow a similar melodic shape to bars 1–2?

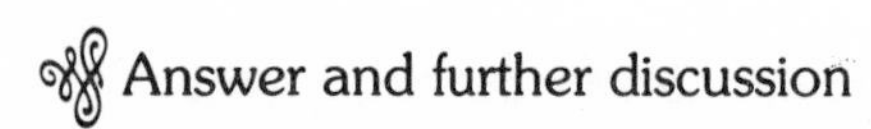

Answer and further discussion

Yes. A nice simple answer! The second phrase does indeed follow the same basic shape. Here are the two phrases:

Figure 8

Now here is the melody, with the pitch contour indicated through the note-heads*.

Figure 9

Exercise

Here is the pitch contour of the two phrases:

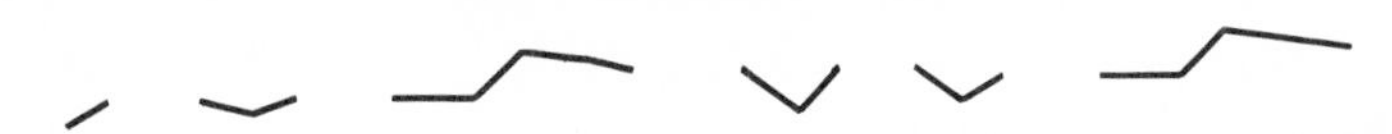

Figure 10

Compare the second phrase with the first. What are the differences, and can you think of a reason for them?

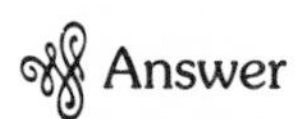

Answer

There are two differences. Most obviously, the second phrase rises higher than the first. Notice also, however, that the leaps and dips in the second phrase are larger than in the first: the intervals (differences in pitch) have been 'opened out.'

I would suggest that the differences are there to give *something extra* to the second phrase. As I hinted before, too much repetition may in itself be rather dangerous: the variations in the second phrase are essential to maintain and increase the musical interest in view of the repetition of both rhythm and general melodic shape. You might well recall, in this connection, the variations in the repeated phrases of 'Amazing Grace' and 'Hey Bo Diddley' in Unit 7.

2.4 HARMONY AND STRUCTURE

Even now we have not quite finished with these four bars. The pattern put forward by the rhythm and the melody is reinforced by the harmony. Among the most important contributions of the harmony are the *cadences* at the end of each phrase. You met the word 'cadence' in Unit 7 when studying 'Amazing Grace' (section 6, p. 26), in that case referring to melodic cadences. The word is also applied to harmony that performs or reinforces the same task: in that sense a cadence is an arrangement of chords which marks the end of a phrase and at the same time signals the phrase's function. Although it would be rather complicated to describe exactly the harmony of Schumann's cadences, their *effects* are easy to recognize.

Listen to example 5, noticing how the harmony reinforces the phrase endings in the accompanied version.

Returning to our literary/verbal parallel, an obvious comparison might be made between cadences and punctuation marks. The first phrase ends with an

*There's a little problem three notes from the end, where Schumann gives two notes in the melody at the same time, but I've chosen the one that I think is most prominent.

'unfinished' cadence: the harmony tells us 'go on – something else is about to happen'. It demands a completion, which is given by the second phrase. The cadence at the end of the second phrase sounds more final.

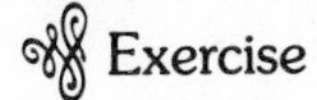

Exercise

You could describe the structure of these four bars by analogy with different types of sentences. Remember that the four bars consist of two 'sentences'. Bearing in mind the parallel I made just now, what description would be appropriate?

Listen again to example 5 before answering.

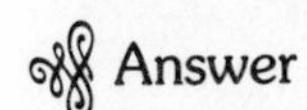

Answer

Question and answer. The first two bars present the 'question' phrase, the continuation being by way of an 'answer' or 'fulfilment'.

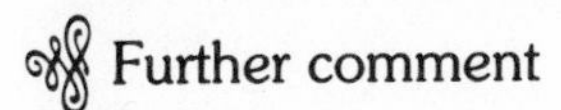

Further comment

Already you should be able to see that there are two 'layers' to these four bars. Each 2–bar phrase has a structure (? – ?? – !), and the four bars taken together also have a structure (? – !). We could represent the whole section thus:

? —— ?? —— ! ? —— ?? —— !
? — !

Figure 11

2.5 FORM

So far we have built up our word equivalents (rhythms, pitch-intervals) into a complete musical sentence. Now let us attempt the perspective of a complete paragraph. In this context, since 'Aveu' is so short, this means the complete movement.

The complete piece is 12 bars long, not counting the repeats. We have accounted for 4 of these bars in some detail. I am now going to represent the complete movement with a diagram. It is a little difficult to square 'movement in time' (which is how music moves) with 'movement in space' (which is how this must be shown in a diagram). However, I'm sure that you will immediately see the point of reflecting the proportions of the movement by a similar area on the page. I will call the opening phrases 'X' and 'Y'. Together they make up the first section, which I will call 'A'. So the diagram looks like this:

X Y
A

Figure 12

I will add one more thing to the diagram for you. After the 'double bar' – that is, at the start of the second section, Schumann continues with a 4-bar musical unit that I shall call 'B'.

So the diagram now looks like this:

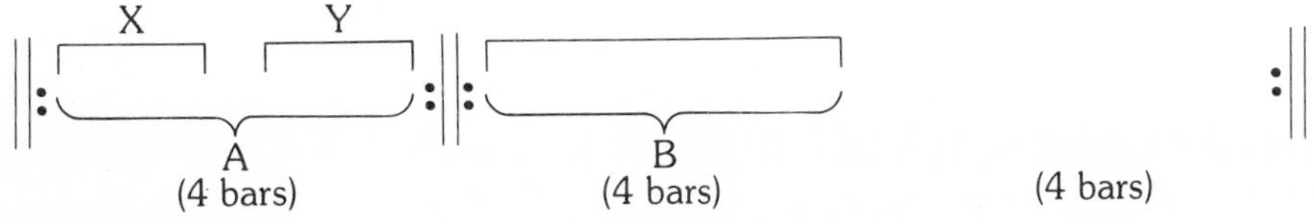

Figure 13

That leaves 4 bars to be accounted for at the end. I want you to fill in the blank space there, after you have listened to the complete piece. You could use either example 1 or example 2 on your tape for this: you may find example 2 easier to follow, as the sections are identified for you.

Exercise

Find the place on the tape, play the complete piece through a couple of times, and then try to fill in the rest of the diagram from what you have heard.

Answer

I hope that you were able to recognize two things:

1 that the tune of the opening four bars 'A', returned at the end of the second section, and

2 that the four bars with which you are now so familiar returned in full, without any omissions, and without any further developments. Your diagram should therefore look like this:

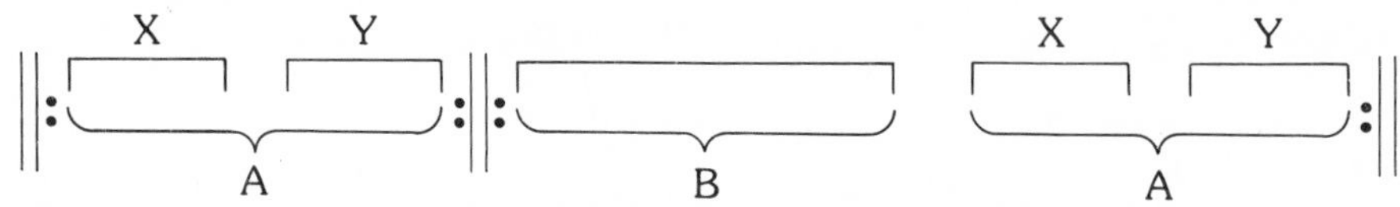

Figure 14

If you managed this answer, well done. If not, please play the complete piece again and listen hard, following my diagram.

Exercise

Let us now concentrate on the 4-bar phrase that I have called 'B'. It does not break up very well into 'X' and 'Y' phrases, but is built from repetitions of a small rhythmic unit.

Listen to the complete piece again (use tape examples 1 or 2), concentrating this time on the 'B' phrase. What can you tell me about

1 the rhythm of 'B' in relation to 'A'

2 the shape of the melody?

Answer

1 The repeated rhythm is the same as that of bar 1, the very opening of the piece:

Figure 15

2 The melody begins with a leap upwards (again a reference to bar 1?), but after that it moves downwards by step. In fact, the melody is a simple descending scale, but with a little 'wiggle' where it leads back into the tune. The pitch contour of the 'B' phrase is therefore:

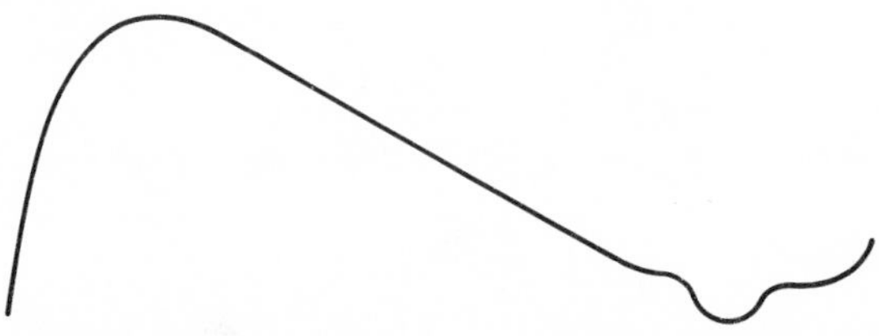

Figure 16

Further comment

In a moment I want you to listen yet again, once more concentrating on the 'B' phrase. This is also rather carefully constructed. 'B' refers to the 'A' section in its rhythm, but in other ways it aims to be rather different. In particular, it avoids the jagged melodic contours of the 'A' section. You could make out a good case for regarding the whole of 'B' as a preparation for the return of the tune! Not only does it lead back gracefully with that 'wiggle' at the end of the scale, but harmony again assists the general enterprise. There is no 'finalizing' cadence at the end, because the harmony leads us back into the opening tune. Throughout the 'B' phrase, as the melody falls, the bass (lowest) part of the harmony gradually rises: they close in to lead back into 'A'. I suggest that this might be an appropriate diagram for the main features of the complete piece:

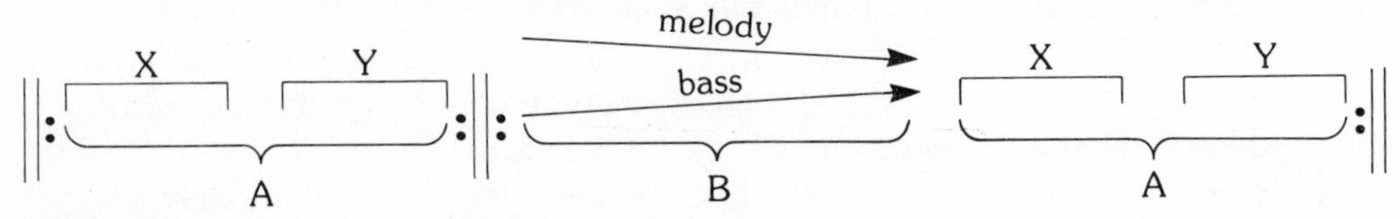

Figure 17

Listening to 'Aveu' complete

Now play the piece through again with these points in mind. Follow figure 17 through as you play it.

'Aveu' is printed in full on p. 78 at the end of the block. You might like to try and follow the music with that as well: this activity is optional, but you may find it easier than you expect, if you are willing to make the attempt.

2.6 A COMPARISON WITH LANGUAGE

In studying 'Aveu' we have gradually progressed from single elements (rhythm, melody), through phrase-structure and cadences, to the organization of the complete piece – the 'form'. This form, as should be clear from the last diagram, has a plan A–B–A: you might even summarize it as 'do something/do something else/go back to your first idea'. It is conveniently described as 'Ternary Form' and it is a scheme that has been followed successfully by many composers, often for pieces very much larger than 'Aveu'. Of course it is not the *only* possible scheme: don't expect every piece of music (even by Schumann) to be in ternary form! However, I think it is most important that you recognize, from your study of 'Aveu', that music *can have a structure* – it does not just 'go on'. The most obvious landmarks by which you can grasp musical structures are elements of repetition – in the case of 'Aveu', the return of a tune. Whether you are consciously aware of it or not, form plays a very important part in guiding your reaction to music. You may, for example, have at some time been attracted to a piece of music by a graceful melody or by a novel *timbre*, only to find that your interest gradually petered out as nothing seemed to 'happen' afterwards: the organization of the total piece was not such as to keep your interest alive. Just as elements of rhythm, melody, harmony and so on contribute to phrases and themes, so themes contribute to larger forms.

You can, in fact, regard musical composition as an art of *elaboration*. Another parallel with language suggests itself here. Schumann's first two bars might be compared to:

> To be, or not to be: that is the question.

Schumann elaborates these two bars into a twelve-bar piece, in just the same way as Shakespeare extends the thought of his original line:

> To be, or not to be: that is the question.
> Whether 'tis nobler in the mind to suffer
> The slings and arrows of outrageous fortune,
> Or to take arms against a sea of troubles,
> And by opposing end them? To die; to sleep;
> No more; and by a sleep to say we end
> The heart-ache and the thousand natural shocks
> That flesh is heir to, 'tis a consummation
> Devoutly to be wished.

Even at this stage, I have only quoted about a third of Shakespeare's composition on the theme 'To be or not to be'. Both compositions have been taken from larger contexts. Schumann's 'Aveu', although a complete piece in itself, is taken from a larger set of piano pieces. Hamlet's soliloquy is only part of one scene from one act of Shakespeare's play.

I used the soliloquy as a comparison for the art of elaboration: if we want to consider the *structure* of Schumann's piece, another parallel with the spoken word suggests itself to me - the art of rhetoric. This parallel seems particularly interesting and appropriate because music and rhetoric both deal in things that are *heard*, and tend to be persuasive in so far as they are coherent. The art of rhetoric can be traced back to the Greeks, and probably originated with the need to present a persuasive case in the law courts:

> The development of Greek oratory into an art form seems to have been strongly influenced by the institution in the fifth century of large democratic juries before whom an artistically developed and uninterrupted speech was possible and even necessary. (George Kennedy, *The Art of Rhetoric in the Roman World, 300 BC – AD 300*, p. 8)

Very soon the orators hit on a recipe for an effective speech. The arrangement or structure of a speech became a matter for textbooks and four 'parts' became standard practice:

1 Introduction;
2 Narration, the exposition of the background and factual details of the case;
3 Proof, the argument based on information given in the narration;
4 Epilogue or Conclusion, consisting of a recapitulation of the case and an emotional appeal to stir the audience.

Look back at the overall plan for the form of 'Aveu' (figure 17). How close is the resemblance to the rhetorical structure just described? (One sentence for similarities, one for differences will be sufficient.)

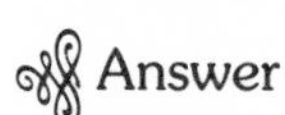

The structure of 'Aveu' is comparable to items 2–4 in the list: bars 1–4 'Narration' (theme A), bars 5–8 'Proof' (because the 'B' section extends the 'argument' of the first bar of the theme), bars 9–12 'Epilogue' (recapitulation of theme A).

Item 1 of the list does not fit, nor can we recognize the second part of item 4 as a separate musical event.

2.7 CONCLUSION TO SECTION 2

The art of rhetoric spread from Greece to Rome, but thereafter the influence of the theorists waned until the revival of interest in Classical learning that we generally describe as the Renaissance. In this respect, there was no more thoroughly 'Renaissance' institution in outlook than the members of the Florentine Camerata, who invented opera* around the year 1600. Rhetorical structure may have exerted a direct influence on the musical forms that they devised for opera, and this in turn probably filtered down as an influence to later music, including even the symphony. However, I am less concerned with the literal and direct influence of rhetorical plans than with the general parallel. Composers attempt convincing structures of musical elaboration and argument in just the same way as speech-makers. Sometimes they even follow a fairly exact parallel to the Classical rhetorical plan. Obviously it depends on the needs of a particular piece of music. Schumann's is so short that he would have been unwise to cram in all of the rhetorical plan, even if he had wanted to: you cannot do everything in 12 bars!

**Opera (which will be mentioned again in the next unit) may be described briefly as 'a drama performed through music'.*

3 VALSE ALLEMANDE

For a final exercise in this section, I want you to try out your skills of 'structural recognition' on another piece from *Carnaval.* 'Valse Allemande' ('German Waltz') also has two repeated sections. As example 6 on band 2 you will find the first section of 'Valse Allemande', including its repeat, and then, after a pause, the whole movement.

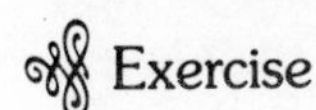

Exercise

Play example 6 through twice, and then try to answer the following questions:

1 What is the structure of this piece?

2 Is this similar to 'Aveu'?

3 In what important respect is the structure different from that of 'Aveu'? (Hint: think carefully about the end of the first section.)

Answers

1 A–B–A (or Ternary) form. The second section begins with new material, but leads back into the opening theme.

2 Yes, very similar.

3 In 'Aveu' the theme was repeated (or recapitulated) exactly in the closing bars of the piece. In 'Valse Allemande' the end of the theme is altered: at the end of the first section it ends quietly and gracefully, but at the end of the second section it ends brusquely.

Further discussion

Well done if you managed the last answer! If you did not, play the movement through again and listen for this feature.

We have not quite finished. 'Valse Allemande' does not stand by itself in 'Carnaval', but is associated with the movement immediately following, 'Paganini'. The complete 'Valse Allemande/Paganini' sequence is example 7 on your tape.

Exercise

Play example 7, 'Valse Allemande/Paganini', and then comment on the overall form of these two movements, taken together.

Answer

The two movements form one larger Ternary (A–B–A) structure, because 'Valse Allemande' is recapitulated at the end of 'Paganini'. So, altogether, there is one big ternary form, but the 'A' section is also itself in ternary form. Like this:

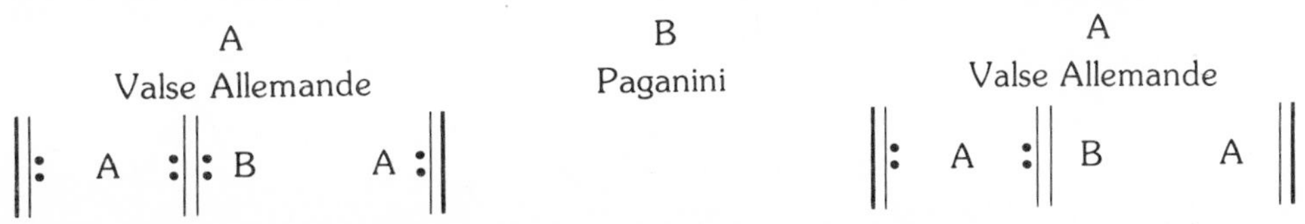

A — Valse Allemande: ||: A :||: B A :||

B — Paganini

A — Valse Allemande: ||: A :|| B A ||

Figure 18

4 CONCLUSION

My dictionary defines 'syntax' as:

> Sentence construction; the grammatical arrangement of words in speech, or writing; set of rules governing this. (*Concise Oxford Dictionary*)

I hope that, looking back over your work on 'Aveu', you will see the point of the parallel with musical composition. Schumann uses rhythm and melody to shape his phrases, and harmony to give a pattern to the phrases: the elements reinforce one another, just as parts of speech 'agree' to make the meaning of a sentence explicit. Beyond syntax we looked at structure, at the overall arrangement of two pieces of music. I do not want to push the parallel with rhetoric too far, but nevertheless I suggest that this is a good way of understanding the larger concept of composition in music. Of course it is true that we have been looking at short, relatively easily grasped, pieces of music. Nevertheless, the principles of structure and syntax that you have encountered in this section are just as relevant to the larger musical forms and are not much more difficult to discern.

Although 'Aveu' and 'Valse Allemande' are complete pieces in themselves, they are also part of a larger work, the collection of about twenty piano pieces forming *Carnaval.* Similarly, I mentioned that Hamlet's soliloquy was only part of a scene, an act, a play. In the next unit we shall proceed to two larger musical *genres* comparable to the 'play' – symphony and oratorio. In so doing we shall continue the process of elaboration we have already followed in this unit from individual elements to larger structures. It would be an interesting debating point as to whether big structures are in some way more impressive creations than small ones: how do you compare a sonnet with a play, a miniature with a mural, a small piano piece with a symphony? I do not wish to imply a value judgement by progressing from the small (piano piece) to the large (symphony, oratorio). Nevertheless, the larger and more complex musical forms provide some of the most rewarding materials for study yet produced by our Western Civilization.

It is vital that you do not lose track of the listening techniques that you have developed in this unit. I suggest, therefore, that before proceeding to Unit 9 *Composer and Audience* you look back over what you have done and, at the least, play through 'Aveu' a couple more times with the movement plan in front of you.

REFERENCE

G. Kennedy (1972) *The Art of Rhetoric in the Roman World 300 BC to AD 300,* Princeton University Press.

Unit 9

COMPOSER AND AUDIENCE

Prepared by Donald J. Burrows for the Course Team

1 INTRODUCTION

This unit is concerned with the large musical genres of symphony and oratorio. You may find these names a little daunting, perhaps because of their foreign origins (in fact, 'Symphony' is the English form of an Italian word). It is as well to begin by admitting that there are difficulties with these words because they are not susceptible to easy definitions. The diversity in the musical pieces that have gone by the names of symphony and oratorio is such that it is very difficult to make generalizations about them. However, this problem is no more serious than it would be in the case of words such as 'chair' or 'table': chairs and tables also exist in many shapes, sizes, styles and materials. The forms of symphony and oratorio have histories of about 250 and 400 years respectively and the musical content of individual examples is considerably determined by matters of time and place. As composer, performer or listener, your notion of what a symphony was depended on when and where you lived. This unit is not simply about 'The Symphony' or 'The Oratorio', but rather seeks to examine particular examples in their historical contexts. Nevertheless, just as an examination of individual pieces of furniture would clarify your idea of what chairs and tables are (if you did not know before, that is), so I hope that your experience with the music of these examples will give you an introduction to features that are common to most symphonies and oratorios.

There are several ways of approaching the study of a musical composition. You may already have guessed, from my description of the contents of this unit as an examination of 'particular examples in their historical contexts', that we shall be attempting to combine and relate two lines of approach. First, building on your experience from the exercises in the previous units, we shall be investigating the musical structure and content of our musical examples, to see how they 'work' as compositions. Secondly, we shall refer each example to the circumstances for which it was composed, paying particular attention to the way the work was received (and anticipated) by its original audience. You will probably recognize from these descriptions that they are examples of the approaches that Richard Middleton described as 'formalist' and 'referentialist' in section 5 of Unit 7.

The relationships between composers and their audiences are usually rather complex, and we need to be cautious about drawing simple causal connections between, say, stylistic features in the music and the social ambience of the original audiences. Nevertheless it is rare for compositions in elaborate forms, such as the symphony and the oratorio, to be undertaken without the expectation of a performance and, consequently, of a specific audience. It does sometimes happen that composers never hear their music performed (Schubert's 'Unfinished' symphony is one famous case), but this circumstance usually arises because a planned performance does not come to fruition or because a composer becomes dissatisfied with his own work, rather than because no performance was envisaged. In considering the influence of the audience on a musical composition it is not really appropriate to adopt a narrow definition of 'audience' along the lines of 'those people whose only involvement with a performance is as listeners'. A private performance of a string quartet or a modern recording session may have no audience in this conventional sense, yet the function of an audience is nevertheless exercised – by performers, recording engineers, or the purchasers of the records. A rather better definition of the audience for our purpose would be something like 'those by whom a composition was intended to be received'.

The audience, thus broadly defined, is of course only one of the influences that may affect composition. For the music that we shall be studying, the influence of *genre* is also particularly important: composers wrote symphonies and oratorios against a background of experiences of previous examples of these forms. These two influences interact: audiences also have experience of previous works in the same *genres*, and consequent expectations. There are also a number of individual factors especially influencing each composition: the available performers, the needs of a particular occasion or, in the case of an opera or oratorio, the words supplied by the librettist, to take three obvious examples. According to circumstances, these various influences could act as stimulants or limitations. They help us to understand the background against which composers made specifically musical choices about style and structure.

As well as forming the conclusion of the *Introduction to Music*, this unit also provides background material that should help you in the second, interdisciplinary, half of the course. This unit introduces you to the Symphony through contrasted examples of the form from 1771, 1808 and 1830: in Unit 25 you will be dealing with a later example of the symphony, from the 1880s. In this unit we shall be examining Handel's *Messiah* in the context of its first performances in the eighteenth century: in Unit 25 we shall see how *Messiah* was performed in very different circumstances in the nineteenth century.

2 THREE SYMPHONIES

2.1 BACKGROUND TO THE SYMPHONY *GENRE*

'Since the time of Haydn, the word has ordinarily indicated an orchestral work of a serious nature and a substantial size'. Such is the diversity in the pieces of music that have been called symphonies that it is difficult to give a general definition, but this one (by Arthur Jacobs in *A New Dictionary of Music*) is as good a starting point as any. They key word is 'orchestral' – it is music for a group of instruments, played together. But not just any randomly-assembled collection of instruments. Orchestral concerts developed through particular institutional circumstances and through particular traditions of instrumental playing that regarded stringed instruments of the violin type (violin, viola, 'cello) as the core of the ensemble.

We perhaps take the existence of orchestras and orchestral concerts for granted. Advertisements for public concerts are readily accessible through posters and newspapers and the sound of an orchestra has become familiar, even to many people who have never seen one 'live', through the medium of sound recording. It may come as something of a surprise, therefore, to discover that the orchestra originated not as an independent institution but as an adjunct to something else. The first orchestras in the modern sense were assembled in the seventeenth century to accompany the singers in the opera house. (An opera house is a theatre in which operas – dramas sung to music – are performed.) The word 'symphony' itself derives from opera: it was applied to more or less any music that the orchestra played when the singers were not singing. This could mean the instrumental introductions or conclusions to songs, or more substantial pieces played to introduce scenes and cover changes of scenery.

As instrumentalists worked together regularly and frequently in the opera house, the orchestral ensemble developed a certain independent momentum. In the second half of the seventeenth century orchestras and orchestral leaders began to gain attention. In France, Louis XIV's court orchestra developed one characteristic style of string playing, under the training of Jean-Baptiste Lully. This orchestra nevertheless remained wedded to the accompaniment of ballets, operas and church music. In Italy, where opera houses were more numerous, there were also opportunities for orchestras to be heard separately. In Bologna orchestral music was performed in church (at the Basilica of San Petronio) on feast days, and in Rome wealthy patrons gave 'secular academies' (private concerts) including orchestral pieces. Violin-playing and violin-making were expanding industries in Italy at this period, and throughout the eighteenth century there was a heavy demand throughout Europe for Italian players and Italian instruments. There were many fine violinists, but the reputation of Arcangelo Corelli as a player, orchestral leader and composer is particularly important. From about 1685 he worked in Rome, producing concerts there for Queen Christina of Sweden and Cardinal Ottoboni. In direct contrast to Lully, Corelli composed no operas. But the fame of his Roman orchestra, and of the music (which he called 'concertos') that he composed for it, spread throughout Europe. The concertos were published in Amsterdam soon after his death in 1714 and they found a ready market: they may, in fact, be regarded as the first 'bestseller' in instrumental music. This was partly because of the expectations aroused by Corelli's reputation, and partly because the concertos contained music in a straightforward, attractive style that was not too difficult to perform. It was rewarding music for both listeners and performers – just the thing for orchestral concerts, in fact.

Who wanted to buy and perform this music? In what circumstances, apart from those already mentioned, did performances of orchestral works take place? In Britain there were some concert-giving clubs in the eighteenth century, often mixing amateur and professional players for orchestral items. In London leading singers and instrumentalists enjoyed 'benefit nights' at the theatre or opera house, the programmes for which usually included orchestral items. Public concerts began in France in 1725 with the foundation of the *Concerts Spirituels*, originally for the performance of sacred music, but soon including orchestral music in the programmes. However, in the area of Europe where the greatest number of eighteenth-century orchestras flourished – northern Italy, Germany, Austria, Czechoslovakia and Hungary – orchestral performances developed under courtly patronage. The richer and more ambitious royal and princely courts maintained a complete opera house with a resident orchestra; the less well-endowed courts ran to a small orchestra with as many string players as could be afforded and perhaps a couple of oboe or horn players. There were a few travelling *virtuosi*, but the majority of the musicians in court orchestras were employed as permanent court servants. The desire to maintain an orchestra may be attributed to attempts to imitate the French court, but the prevailing musical style was Italian, with a steady demand for Italian string players. There was no doubt a certain rivalry between the courts for the services of the best musicians. Court music was in the hands of a resident player-composer, styled *Kapellmeister* or *Konzertmeister* in the German-speaking countries. Haydn and Mozart, the greatest symphony composers of the eighteenth century, spent considerable parts of their careers working within the courtly system; Beethoven was the son of a court musician.

The symphony developed in response to a need for new music in the mid-eighteenth century as orchestral performances grew more popular. In addition to specially-composed pieces, usually called by the old name 'concertos', the repertory was extended with orchestral pieces taken from operatic (or opera-style) works – hence the appearance of the word 'symphony'. The most extensive symphonies within operas normally came at the beginning, serving as overtures before the drama on stage began, and these could be extracted as concert items. They usually consisted of a succession of pieces of music at contrasting speeds – 'movements'. The style and plan of these symphonies provided materials for the further development of concert works along similar lines. It is difficult to make generalizations about the earliest experiments, but by the 1770s we would expect most symphonies to have four movements:

1 Fast (this is sometimes preceded by a slow introduction in symphonies from the later part of the period.)

2 Slow

3 Minuet (a moderate-speed dance-derived movement)

4 Fast

This, of course, only describes the external scheme of the music. Many factors contributed to make the symphony a particularly rich musical form. Let us now look more closely at one movement from a relatively early symphony.

2.2 A SALZBURG SYMPHONY BY MOZART

Like Beethoven, Wolfgang Amadeus Mozart (1756–91) was the son of a court musician. His father, Leopold, was a violinist at the court of the Prince-Archbishop of Salzburg, and enjoyed a modestly successful career there, becoming *Vize-Kapellmeister* (Vice-Kapellmeister) in 1763. Fortunately his employer at this period was fairly easy going and allowed Leopold time away from court to take his musically talented children around Europe. No doubt, in addition to genuine pride in Wolfgang's musical talent and a desire to broaden his education, Leopold hoped that the contacts made on these tours would be helpful when his son eventually needed a job. From Leopold's later letters we know that he attached some importance to Wolfgang gaining a good safe position, preferably at one of the more prestigious courts.

In December 1771 father and son returned to Salzburg from a visit to Italy. Soon after their return the Prince-Archbishop died. His successor was known from the start to be a difficult man to please. Nevertheless, in the absence of any other immediate opening, a job at Salzburg was not to be despised. Wolfgang was appointed *Konzertmeister* in July 1772, with a modest annual salary. Between December 1771 and August 1772 he composed eight symphonies. While it would be beyond the evidence to suggest that these gained Mozart his post at Salzburg, we can be sure that they were composed for performance there, and were taken as proofs of his competence. The Symphony in A major from which our case study is taken was the first of this series, finished on 30 December 1771, about a month before Mozart's sixteenth birthday.

 Exercise

Find the recording of the first movement of the symphony (cassette 3, side 2, band 3.) Take a counter reading so that you can find the start of the movement easily when I ask you to replay the movement.

Let us concentrate on general impressions first. Play the opening (about 30 seconds of music will be fine) and then decide which of the following descriptions applies to the style of the music:

elegant, violent, rough, song-like, dissonant

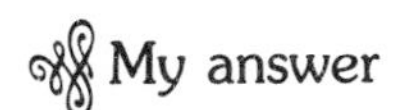 My answer

I would have chosen 'elegant' and 'song-like'. The style of Mozart's melodies ('song-like') and harmonies (definitely not, in conventional terms, 'dissonant' in this extract) is smooth and well balanced. We'll return to the implications of this later. Meanwhile, let us turn our attention to his use of the orchestra.

 Exercise

For the next exercises I am going to give timings (to the nearest second) of things to listen for. A watch or clock that shows seconds (not necessarily a stop-watch) will help you to focus accurately on the musical landmarks. Listen again to the opening of the symphony, paying attention to Mozart's use of the orchestra. Listen particularly carefully to the change in texture that happens at the end of the tune, 13 seconds from the beginning.

Exercise

Describe as accurately as you can what happens at that point, and the contrast in Mozart's use of the instruments.

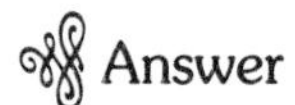
Answer

Mozart begins with just a few instruments (violins). At the end of the theme he brings in the full orchestra.

Exercise

Now listen to that again. What new instruments can you hear when the full orchestra enters? (I don't expect you to name *all* of them: concentrate on the instruments which sound distinctly different from those you heard at the very opening.)

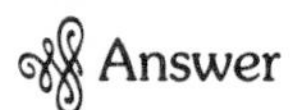
Answer

When the full orchestra entered, you should have noticed the lower-pitched string instruments ('cellos, double basses) coming in below the violins: they were not there before. Also you hear the wind instruments for the first time: the flutes can be heard joining in with the tune.

Further comment

If you listened to the full 30 seconds, you probably noticed that another different orchestral colour entered at about 25 seconds – the horns. The order of events, therefore, is:

0'0" violins

0'13" full strings, flutes

0'25" horns join in

Listen once more to the extract, and see if you can recognize these orchestral colours.

Exercise

In a moment I am going to ask you to listen to a slightly longer extract, this time concentrating on the themes (or tunes). Mozart builds this movement around two main tunes that I shall call 'X' and 'Y'. The opening tune we shall call 'X'. Now, listen to about two minutes of the movement and fill in the blanks in this list:

0'0" Tune X

0'58" Tune

1'40" Tune

Answer

0'0" Tune X

0'58" Tune Y

1'40" Tune X

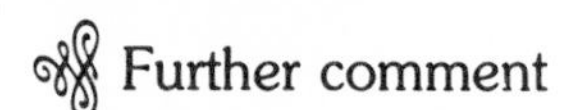
Further comment

I hope that you found that easy. After the previous exercises, you should have been familiar with Tune X, and it is fairly easy to recognize because it is played by violins alone. (Tune Y uses more of the orchestra.) If you did not get the answer, or found it difficult, do re-play the extract once more, listening out for the tunes at the right moment.

The reappearance of Tune X at 1'40" should have given you an important message: that this movement is organized in a deliberately planned structure. There is more to the movement than the elegant language and the varied orchestration. I am now going to ask you to try to follow the structure of the complete movement by recognizing the appearances of the main themes.

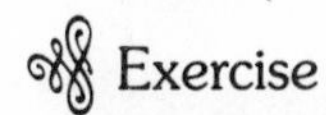

Exercise

Play the complete movement through twice, with your watch/clock to hand. Your timings may vary slightly depending on your tape-playing equipment and your initial reaction time. You can tell if you are 'fast' or 'slow' from the 'End' timing and adjust accordingly at the second hearing.

Fill in the blanks on the following table. (You needn't wait for the movement to finish – write down the identity of the tune as soon as you recognize it.) There are three possible answers for each of the blanks: Tune X, Tune Y or New Tune.

0'00" Tune X	3'21"
0'58" Tune Y	3'54"
1'40" Tune X	4'54"
2'38"	5'37" End

Answer

0'00" Tune X	3'21" New Tune
0'58" Tune Y	3'54" Tune X
1'40" Tune X	4'54" Tune Y
2'38" Tune Y	5'37" End

If you managed that, well done! If not, try again, listening with the answers in front of you. Remember – it should be easy to recognize Tune X because of the thinner texture of the violins alone.

Exercise

Look at the previous answer. What pattern do you see to the structure?

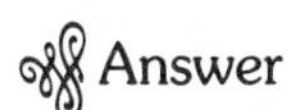

Answer

It is based on the alteration of Tunes X and Y: they appear three times successively, always in the order XY.

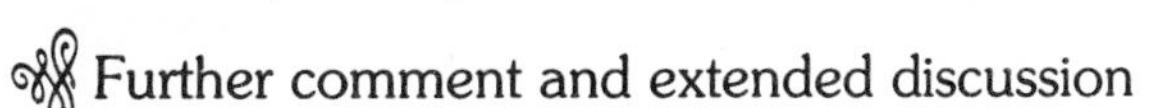

Further comment and extended discussion

I shall re-arrange the plan of the themes into the style of the diagrams that we used in Unit 8 Part II, thus:

X Y X Y New X Y

Figure 1

In fact, I can simplify this diagram a little more, because the opening section of it is repeated exactly. (I would not expect you necessarily to have recognized this.) Thus:

Figure 2

You might have spotted that this diagram looks rather like that of 'Aveu' (Unit 8, Part II, p. 44) which was:

Figure 3

My comment would be that it is similar in some ways, but that in others it is not. The Mozart movement introduces a new complication into the scheme, because Tunes X and Y are presented in different *keys* in the opening section, but return in the same key at the end – so they are not exactly identical in the way that the 'A' sections of 'Aveu' were. A more refined plan of Mozart's movement would therefore look like this:

Figure 4

You do not need to understand the technicalities of 'keys' at foundation level, but you might possibly be aware of the effect of a different key on the 'Y' tune, which is played at a higher pitch level in the first section than at the end. There's also a very important effect on the 'non-tune' parts of the plan, because the music between X and Y in the first section has to *change* key, while in the final section it remains in the same key.

I'll emphasize again, however, that you are not required to 'know about keys' or to recognize the sound of different keys at this stage. The point is that, although Mozart's XY sections are identical as to *themes*, they differ in other ways. So, while the plans of 'Aveu' and Mozart's movement have some specific similarities, they are not identical, because Schumann's 'A' is not exactly comparable to Mozart's 'XY'. These differences in fact mean that the Mozart movement is in a rather more complex form that cannot simply be described as 'Ternary'.

The important thing that the two pieces have in common, however, is that they both *have a plan*, and that the recurrence of themes is an important signal that will help you to follow the plan. Mozart's movement follows a plan that we call *Sonata Form*. It is a design that composers have found particularly stimulating for instrumental music, and one that allows many subtle variations.

2.3 'MEANING' IN MOZART'S SYMPHONY

Play the Mozart movement through one last time. Then attempt to answer (in not more than two sentences!) the question 'What is this music about?'

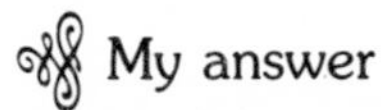

It is 'about' the musical aspects that we have identified and examined in the previous exercises: elegantly-expressed, balanced musical phrases; imaginative use of the orchestra; a carefully-organized and satisfying overall structure.

Further comment

You may have thought that this trick question – or perhaps that I gave an evasive answer. I suppose that an alternative way of answering would have been a negative one – that the music refers to nothing outside the music. The music, being purely instrumental, carries no verbal message. As far as we can tell, Mozart was not intending to convey a specific scene, story or event. We could make up a story to go with the music, of course, but we could not pretend that that was Mozart's intention. Is this answer sufficient, though? Could we argue that the music is 'meaning-less'? We might, perhaps, argue that the very ease, balance and grace of the music is self-defeating: that the music recedes too easily from our attention and that it is easy to take for granted because it sounds conventional or polite – just the sort of thing for a court audience in fact. Such an argument would be about *style* as much as *content*. The music could be in a much more abrasive style and still carry as little, or as much, 'meaning'.

Mozart's approach to the symphony, one that I would describe as 'Classical', is strongly connected with the 'play' element in human consciousness – the impulse to experiment with and manipulate ideas and objects. This is not to deny that his music can suggest strong emotions, but it is difficult to tie non-verbal music to *specific* emotions. Cross-references between musical content and emotional content are very difficult to make, but they are certainly part of music's 'meaning'. However, I was very careful to ask you 'What is this music about?' and not 'What does this music mean?' – hoping that you would realize, in attempting your answer, that Mozart's music was largely self-referential, and 'about' the music itself.

2.4 THE ROMANTIC ALTERNATIVE: BERLIOZ

To return for a moment to the framework that I put forward in section 1, we might say that the composition of Mozart's symphony was influenced by:

1 The *genre* history of the symphony – i.e. the previous existence of multi-movement works in a similar style and form.

2 The audience, in that the Salzburg court provided the occasion for the performance of symphonies. It is difficult to know whether to relate the elegant style of Mozart's music directly to the tastes of a court audience, but the circumstances of court performance certainly controlled such important factors as the length of the symphony and the orchestra available. The sophisticated plan of sonata form seems to presuppose an audience interested in following the structure, consciously or instinctively. (It's worth bearing in mind the alternative possibility that Mozart's structures were too sophisticated for his audience, but that his music was acceptable merely because it was in an attractive style.)

3 Mozart's own wish to experiment in particular ways with melodies, harmony, orchestration and overall structure.

Mozart's 'Classical' approach to the symphony – the symphony as being primarily concerned with musical matters – might be accounted for under all three headings; it was the approach of earlier symphony (and concerto) composers, it was what the audience expected, and it was one that interested Mozart himself.

For an entirely different approach to the symphony *genre*, we are now going to study an extract from a symphony composed in 1830. In this example the composer definitely intended that the music should be associated with something else – in this case, a story. The approach, one that I would describe as 'Romantic', was particularly characteristic of some nineteenth-century composers who made self-conscious attempts to link music closely with the other arts. Find the extract from the *Symphonie Fantastique* by Hector Berlioz (1803–69) on cassette 3, side 2, band 4, and take a counter reading.

Exercise

Play the extract twice. What scene do you think this depicts, and what incident(s) are represented in the music?

The composer's answer

> The artist, now knowing beyond all doubt that his love is not returned, poisons himself with opium. The dose of the narcotic, too weak to take his life, plunges him into a sleep

> accompanied by the most horrible visions. He dreams that he has killed the woman he loved, and that he is condemned to death, brought to the scaffold, and witnesses *his own execution.* The procession is accompanied by a march that is sometimes fierce and sombre, sometimes stately and brilliant: loud crashes are followed abruptly by the dull thud of heavy footfalls. At the end of the march, the first four bars of the *idée fixe* [a tune representing 'the woman he loved'] recur like a last thought of love interrupted by the fatal stroke (trans. Nicholas Temperley (1972) *Hector Berlioz: The Complete Works*, Vol. 16, p. 218).

Your musical extract came from the end of the movement. Now that you know the composer's intention, play the extract again.

My comments

I think that the important question is not 'did you get the right answer?' but 'does it matter that your answer was not the same as the composer's?' I would be very surprised indeed if your image of what was represented matched the composer's exactly, unless you had known about the symphony previously, that is. Your answer, however wildly different from Berlioz's, might have been one that fitted the music perfectly well: there is no way of reading the composer's mind from the music itself. Berlioz realized this and planned that the audience should have a knowledge of his story *before* hearing the music. Here is his statement of intention, with the original explanatory footnote:

> The composer's intention has been to treat of various states in the life of an artist, in so far as they have musical quality. Since this instrumental drama lacks the assistance of words, an advance explanation of the plan is necessary. The following Programme*, therefore, should be thought of as if it were the spoken text of an opera, serving to introduce the musical movements and to explain their character and expression.

Once you know the story, it is easy to relate the music to it and you could no doubt elaborate the images for yourself – an unruly procession, the moment of concentration before the moment of execution, and then the general hubbub as the head rolls off, possibly into the crowd.

Play the extract once more before proceeding.

Composer and audience

The *Symphonie Fantastique* was composed, and first performed, in Paris. It is hardly possible, knowing this, to hear Berlioz's symphony without remembering the turmoil that had centred on Paris in the sixty years since the date of Mozart's symphony: the French Revolution, followed by the period of the Napoleonic Wars. The symphony itself was caught up in the next round of political turbulence. Berlioz arranged a performance in a Paris theatre (the Théâtre des Nouveautés) for May 1830, but this was cancelled after a couple of chaotic rehearsals, and the first performance eventually took place at the Paris Conservatoire in December. During the intervening six months Paris had seen another uprising, and the December performance was given as a benefit concert for those wounded in the July revolution. Berlioz, in his *Memoirs*, suggests that the novelty of the symphony caused something of a stir, but the first performance was hardly noticed in the newspapers, which were preoccupied with political matters. I would suspect that the performance was regarded at the time as yet another event in a situation already crowded with many excitements. Certainly we can assume that the audience was more lively and volatile than that which had heard Mozart's symphony at Salzburg. Another important consideration is that 'revolutionary' Paris had become a centre for composers, writers and artists, many of whom saw their own activities as experimental and progressive and would have been interested in attempts to link music with literature. The audience at the

**[Berlioz's footnote] 'At concerts at which this symphony is played, the distribution of this Programme to the audience is indispensable to the full understanding of the dramatic plan of the work'.*

symphony's first performance included Franz Liszt, the Hungarian composer and pianist who is now recognized as a major influence in the spread of the 'Romantic' approach among European composers.

It would be very tempting to make up some simple links along these lines:

Mozart = Classical = Aristocratic audience = eighteenth century

Berlioz = Romantic = Revolutionary audience = nineteenth century

In practice, things are not quite so simple. You can find the Romantic approach to instrumental music in composers writing for pre-revolutionary audiences: a symphony based on Ovid's *Metamorphoses* by a composer named Dittersdorf was performed in Vienna before the emperor in 1786, for example, and sixty years previously Vivaldi had composed concertos inspired by sonnets about the four seasons. Conversely, there were some nineteenth-century composers, such as Mendelssohn and Brahms, who maintained a more 'Classical' approach to the symphony than Berlioz. The balance between Romantic and Classical approaches was as much a matter of individual temperaments and interests as of changing historical periods. (Remember that in Unit 7, section 5, Richard Middleton suggested that in general terms these approaches have had a long and concurrent history within European culture.)

Looking at the other side of the picture, it is unwise to generalize about audiences primarily in terms of historical periods. The audiences in 1771 for a symphony at a concert in London or Paris, or at an Italian Academy, would have been rather different from the court audience at Salzburg. The audience at Leipzig (where Felix Mendelssohn worked) in the 1830s was very different from Berlioz's exactly contemporary Parisian audience: it was a rather conservative audience, but one containing many connoisseurs and would-be composers with an appreciation of matters of musical construction in the way of melodies, harmonies and forms. In fact, you might well regard the members of Mendelssohn's audience as being closer to Mozart's in their attitudes, even though the prevailing social ambience was middle-class rather than aristocratic. We therefore have to take individual factors into account which ruin our simple equations. We need to know specific things about both audiences and composers before we can judge the relationship between them. Even then it may be more useful to pursue the investigation in terms of influences and contexts rather then in terms of causes and effects. You may feel that a knowledge of the original audience has not necessarily helped your understanding of the music. If so, I suggest that you try a little experiment. Try to imagine a performance of the *Symphonie Fantastique* at the formal Salzburg court, and then a performance of the Mozart symphony before the rather *avant-garde* Parisian audience in 1830. I think you will quickly realise that the musical and historical images do not fit together so well. You simply would not compose that type of symphony for that type of audience.

The orchestras

Before leaving the examples by Mozart and Berlioz, I would like you to make one direct musical comparison.

Play the Berlioz extract again, followed by about one minute of the Mozart movement. What difference do you notice in the sound of the orchestra? (Give a short general answer, followed by anything that you notice about particular orchestral sounds.)

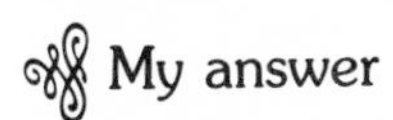

My general answer would be: it sounds as if Berlioz's orchestra is much larger. More particularly, I noticed several instruments that were not present in Mozart's orchestra, especially brass instruments (trumpets, trombones) and percussion (cymbals and drums.)

Further comments

Here again, there are both general and particular points to be considered. It is generally true that composers wrote for larger orchestras in 1830 than in 1771. This was partly a consequence of the changed circumstances in which orchestral music was performed: the size of court orchestras was limited by the number of court servants that the patron could afford to employ, whereas one of the things that attracted audiences to public concerts in theatres or concert halls was the chance of hearing an orchestra of a substantial size. It is also true that most theatres and concert halls were in any case larger than court drawing rooms, and that we should probably view the growth of the 'symphony orchestra' in relation to the orchestras that were regularly employed in the orchestral pits of opera houses. Even so, it is clear that Berlioz was not using a 'typical' orchestra in 1830. One of the reasons that the first performance did not take place as planned was that Berlioz had scored his symphony for an unusually large orchestra. There was a specifically Parisian tradition behind the employment of large musical forces, and the first 'revolutionary period' in the 1790s had seen performances by massed choirs and large military bands. Nevertheless, the size of Berlioz's orchestra created severe practical problems. Here is how he described the problems encountered in the early rehearsals of the *Symphonie Fantastique*:

> The Théâtre des Nouveautés had for some time been performing opéras-comiques, and now had a reasonably good orchestra under the command of Bloc. He persuaded me to offer my new work to the directors of the theatre; we should jointly organize a concert and give the work a hearing. The directors consented, for the sole reason that the symphony's unusual programme had caught their fancy; they thought a lot of people would come out of curiosity. But I wanted a performance on a really grand scale, so I engaged a further eighty players. When added to Bloc's, they formed an orchestra of a hundred and thirty. The theatre had no normal provision for an army of performers on this scale; the necessary physical conditions, the platforms for the different levels, even the desks [music stands], were lacking. To all my inquiries the directors replied with the imperturbable calm of men who have no conception of the difficulties involved: I had no need to worry, everything would be seen to, they had a scene-shifter who was a very clever fellow. But when the day came for the rehearsal, and my orchestra of a hundred and thirty tried to arrange themselves on the stage, there was nowhere to put them. The tiny pit, when pressed into service, barely accommodated the violins. From all over the theatre an uproar arose that would have driven a much more sanguine composer demented. People were calling for desks, while the carpenters strove to knock together something that would do instead. The scene-shifter went about swearing and searching for his flats and struts. There were cries for chairs, for instruments, for candles; the double basses were out of strings; there was no place anywhere for the drums. The orchestral attendant did not know where to begin. Bloc and I were in thirty-seven different places at once; but it was all to no avail. The situation had got beyond control. (*The Memoirs of Hector Berlioz*, trans. David Cairns, pp. 148–9)

This extract reveals not only the experimental nature of Berlioz's large orchestra, but also that the large orchestra was an essential element in Berlioz's plan to startle the audience with a really original work.

A moment ago I mentioned 'a typical orchestra of the 1830s'. Actually, so many different factors are involved that it is difficult to talk about 'typical' orchestras. It is important to realize, however, that the general growth in the size of orchestras was not merely a matter of adding new instruments: trumpets, trombones, drums and so on. These instruments were also occasionally available in the eighteenth century, and were used by composers from time to time. But there was also an increase in the number of instruments of the same type playing the same part. From 1784 we have some figures from the Salzburg court showing that the court employed 12 violinists: Berlioz wanted 'at least 30' violins for his symphony. In each case the violins were divided into two parts, so at Salzburg there might have been 6 violins playing the same part, as against 15 in Paris. A tune played by 15 violins is louder than the same tune played by 6 violins, but, more importantly, the quality of the sound is also different. Extend this difference through other instruments of the orchestra and you will understand one of the reasons why the Berlioz extract sounds so different from the Mozart extract.

The table below shows the size and constitution of orchestras from the eighteenth and nineteenth centuries that were associated with our musical examples and case studies. This is a reference table – you do not have to learn the details! But the examples given there should show you clearly the general trend towards larger orchestras in the nineteenth century.

	Handel: Messiah *Foundling Hospital London 1754*	*Mozart: Salzburg Court Orchestra 1784*	*Berlioz: Symphonie Fantastique Paris 1833*
STRINGS			
Violin 1	14 (Violin 1 and 2)	6	30 (Violin 1 and 2)
Violin 2		6	
Viola	6	1	10
'Cello	3	2	12
Double bass	2	4	9
Harp			2
WOODWIND			
Flute			2 (1 player doubling Piccolo)
Oboe	4	3	2
Cor Anglais			1
Clarinet			2
Bassoon	4	2	4
BRASS			
Horn	2	2	4
Trumpet	2		2
Cornet			1
Trombone		(3*)	3
Ophicleide			2
PERCUSSION			
Timpani	1 (2 drums)		3 (4 drums)
Other percussion, including bells			4
KEYBOARD			
(Harpsichord, organ)	2	3	—
TOTAL	40	29	93

**Trombones were used at Salzburg for church music but not for symphonies.*

1 Foundling Hospital Committee Minutes, 29 May 1754, Thomas Coram Foundation, London

2 Figures from Neal Zaslaw: 'Towards a revival of the classical orchestra', Table 1. p. 176. *Proceedings of the Royal Musical Association* Vol. 103 (1976–77).

3 Concert Programme, 22 December 1833: figures given in Appendix VII of Berlioz: *Symphonie Fantastique* ed. Nicholas Temperley.

2.5 BETWEEN MOZART AND BERLIOZ: BEETHOVEN'S 'PASTORAL' SYMPHONY

In the extract from Berlioz's *Memoirs* quoted in the last section he mentioned that the directors of the theatre were interested in the performance because the symphony's unusual programme 'caught their fancy'. In a preview the day before the first performance of the *Symphonie Fantastique*, a Paris newspaper said 'This is the first time that anyone has thought of giving a precise meaning to instrumental music'. In fact that claim was not quite true. Several previous symphonies had been accompanied by commentaries of some sort from their composers. The most famous of them is the 'Pastoral' Symphony by Ludwig van Beethoven (1770–1827) composed in 1807–8 and first performed in Vienna in 1808. Beethoven intended the symphony to be heard in conjunction with explanatory titles to the movements in the printed programme, and the music contains various descriptive passages. For the last listening exercise in this section I want to concentrate on three of these descriptive passages.

Exercise

Play the three extracts from Beethoven's 'Pastoral' Symphony (cassette 3, side 2, band 5 (a–c)).

After each extract, stop the tape and write down what you think was represented in the music. Remember the symphony's title – the answer will probably be something to do with the rural life. (You may find it helpful to listen to the extracts a couple of times, and I suggest that you make a note of the counter readings at the start of each of the extracts so that you can find them quickly.)

Answers

(a) Birdsong. The higher woodwind instruments (flute, oboe, clarinet) are used to imitate the calls of the nightingale, quail and cuckoo.

(b) A thunderstorm. The opening music is the end of a movement representing 'Peasants merrymaking', and this is suddenly broken off by sounds of distant thunder ('cellos and double basses). A full-orchestra cloudburst recedes, leaving lightning flashes (timpani and woodwind).

(c) This is much more difficult, and if you have not met this symphony before I would be surprised if you came very near the answer. Beethoven's title is 'Awakening of happy feelings on arriving in the country'. You may have an answer that matches the mood that this implies – relaxed, happy, slightly expectant, but don't be discouraged if you did not come very close to Beethoven's title.

Now play the extracts again, with these answers in mind.

Further discussion

I presented these extracts in an order moving from the particular to the general. The first is an example of musical *imitation* – a direct transference of sound impressions into a 'composition'. Of course this is rather contrived – you can only imitate external things which make musically useful noises and even birds do not usually sing the right notes, at the right time, and in the right rhythm, to fit in with a piece of music!

The second example also contains some direct imitation of external sounds – thunder, lightning and, possibly, raindrops. However, this differs from the first example in that it is *dynamic*. An event, not merely a picture, is portrayed. To put it crudely, the music tells some sort of story, and this type of example we could correctly describe as 'programme music'. It is conventionalized, of course: it does not sound *exactly* like a storm, but it represents one in musical terms.

The third example does not attempt to imitate or represent any external object or happening. Instead it portrays an emotion. For that reason it is much less specific than the first two examples and much more difficult to define precisely. Even if I had told you that this music portrays a particular emotion, I do not suppose that the variety in the possible answers would have been much reduced. This is presumably why Beethoven felt the need to make his intentions clear by printing titles to the movements in the programme. Even so, this type of musical representation is necessarily less explicit than the portrayal of bird-song and storms; Beethoven described his symphony as 'more expression of feeling than painting'.

Within the 'Romantic' approach, then, music can make reference to other things in various ways and at various levels. The extreme form of the 'Classical' approach – music that has no reference whatever to anything outside itself – is probably impossible to attain, for even a work like Mozart's symphony will have been affected by such things as the rhythms of dance music or song-phraseology, which is related to literary verse forms. On the other hand, the extreme 'Romantic' approach, where the course of the music is totally controlled by external references, is equally elusive; once into the process of composition, the internal needs for coherence in melodies, forms and so on have a way of taking over the composer's attention. I think that a good argument could be made for the proposition that extra-musical influences (including that of the intended audience) are at their strongest only up to the moment that a composer puts pen to paper.

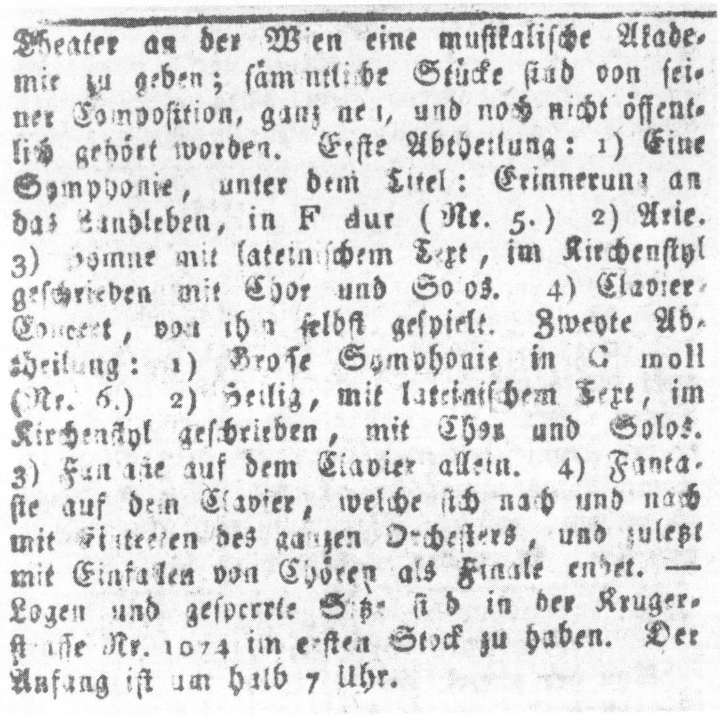

Theater an der Wien eine musikalische Akademie zu geben; sämmtliche Stücke sind von seiner Composition, ganz neu, und noch nicht öffentlich gehört worden. Erste Abtheilung: 1) Eine Symphonie, unter dem Titel: Erinnerung an das Landleben, in F dur (Nr. 5.) 2) Arie. 3) Hymne mit lateinischem Text, im Kirchenstyl geschrieben mit Chor und Solos. 4) Clavier-Concert, von ihm selbst gespielt. Zweyte Abtheilung: 1) Große Symphonie in C moll (Nr. 6.) 2) Heilig, mit lateinischem Text, im Kirchenstyl geschrieben, mit Chor und Solos. 3) Fantasie auf dem Clavier allein. 4) Fantasie auf dem Clavier, welche sich nach und nach mit Eintreten des ganzen Orchesters, und zuletzt mit Einfallen von Chören als Finale endet. — Logen und gesperrte Sitze sind in der Krugerstraße Nr. 1074 im ersten Stock zu haben. Der Anfang ist um halb 7 Uhr.

Figure 5 Part of the Wiener Zeitung *advertisement for Beethoven's 'Akademie': (Photo: Bildarchiv, Österreichische Nationalbibliothek)*

Composer and audience

Read the advertisement for the concert at which the 'Pastoral' symphony was first performed, and the description of the concert from a letter by the composer J. F. Reichardt, who attended the performance (translations below). Then answer in a short paragraph the questions that follow.

Musical Akademie

On Thursday, December 22, Ludwig van Beethoven will have the honour to give a musical *Akademie* int the R.I. Priv. Theater-an-der-Wien. All the pieces are of his composition, entirely new, and not yet heard in public... First Part: 1, A Symphony, entitled: 'A Recollection of Country Life', in F major (No. 5). 2, Aria. 3, Hymn with Latin text, composed in the church style with chorus and solos. 4, Pianoforte Concerto played by himself.

Second Part. 1, Grand Symphony in C minor (No. 6). 2, Holy, with Latin text composed in the church style with chorus and solos. 3, Fantasia for Pianoforte alone. 4, Fantasia for the Pianoforte which ends with the gradual entrance of the entire orchestra and the introduction of choruses as a finale.

Boxes and reserved seats are to be had in the Krugerstrasse No. 1074, first storey. Beginning at half past six o'clock. (*Wiener Zeitung*, December 17, 1808)

Vienna, 25 December 1808

During this past week, when the theatres were closed and the evenings were taken up with musical performances and concerts, my eagerness and resolution to hear everything caused me no small embarrassment. This was particularly the case on the 22nd, because the local musicians gave the first of the season's great musical performances in the Burgtheater for the benefit of their admirable Society for Musicians' Widows; on the same day, however, Beethoven also gave a concert for his own benefit in the large suburban theatre, consisting entirely of his own compositions. I could not possibly miss this and accepted with heartfelt gratitude Prince Lobkowitz's kind invitation to take me with him in his box. There we held out in the bitterest cold from half-past six until half-past ten, and experienced the fact that one can easily have too much of a good – and even more of a strong – thing. I, no more than the extremely kindly and gentle Prince, whose box was in the first tier very near to the stage, on which the orchestra with Beethoven conducting were quite close to us, would have thought of leaving the box before the very end of the concert, although several faulty performances tried our patience to the utmost. Poor Beethoven, for whom this concert provided the first and only small profit that he had been able to earn and retain during this whole year, had encountered a great deal of opposition and very little support both in its organization and performance. The singers and the orchestra were assembled from very heterogeneous elements. Moreover, it had not even been possible to arrange a complete rehearsal of all the pieces to be performed, every one of which was filled with passages of the utmost difficulty. You will be amazed [to hear] all that was performed by this fertile genius and untiring worker, in the course of four hours. (H. C. Robbins Landon, *Beethoven*, p. 127).

Exercise

Were the circumstances closer to those described for the first performance of Mozart's symphony, or of Berlioz's? What were the audience's experiences of the concert? What influences determined the choice of programme?

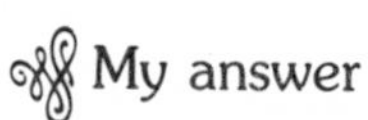

My answer

In most respects, the circumstances were closer to those of the first performance of Berlioz's symphony. The concert was a public one, performed to a paying audience in a theatre: exactly the circumstances that Berlioz anticipated with his public rehearsal. The description of Beethoven's difficulties in assembling and rehearsing the performers is also reminiscent of Berlioz's account of the first rehearsals of his symphony. (By contrast, Mozart's symphony was first perfomed by the court musicians as part of their regular duty – they did not have to be gathered separately.) The audience experienced a four-hour concert, under-rehearsed, in a cold building. The content of the programme was mainly influenced by the composer's need to display his own wares: hence the rather overloaded programme with a mixed bag of church music, piano pieces and an operatic song in addition to two new symphonies*.

Further comment

You may possibly have been slightly confused when trying to answer the last exercise by the mention of a Prince (Lobkowitz) in the audience for Beethoven's concert: doesn't that sound more like the Mozart performance? In fact circumstances in Vienna were rather exceptional, for the city of the Imperial court was a home for many of the lesser nobility. There would have been nothing unusual in a Prince attending a public concert, and in fact Beethoven relied on this type of musically-orientated patron for support, even though he was not directly employed in a court post that made demands comparable to Mozart's.

**When the symphonies were published, their numbers were reversed: the 'Pastoral' symphony is therefore now known as 'No. 6'. Beethoven had worked at the composition of the two symphonies concurrently, a frequent practice with him.*

Nevertheless, although we can talk about 'the orchestra' as a musical institution that would have been understood by 1808, neither Beethoven nor Berlioz worked within a system of regular public concert seasons. Although any concert promoter of today would immediately see the folly of putting on a four-hour, under-rehearsed programme in a cold building, Beethoven's circumstances do not provide an exact parallel to modern conditions. Beethoven needed a benefit night devoted to his music to ensure that his new music gained a hearing on his own terms. On the night he appeared as composer, conductor and solo pianist. The timing of the benefit concert was controlled by the dates that Beethoven was allowed the use of the theatre, and the availability of sufficient willing performers. In such circumstances there was no question of making a regular living by mounting public concerts of orchestral music.

3 AN ORATORIO: HANDEL'S *MESSIAH*

3.1 INTRODUCTION

In considering the interaction of composer and audience in the creation of new musical works we are mainly concerned with the first performances of the works involved, and their original audiences. However, the desire to maintain or revive performances of some works from previous generations has been a noticeable characteristic of musical communities in Europe during the last two centuries. (Here I am referring to organized public performances of music for their own sake; in the context of religious services continuous performance traditions go back much further, and there are also several other traditions involving the oral transmission of both sacred and secular music through successive generations.)

In Unit 25 you will be studying the way that Handel's oratorios were performed at the Crystal Palace in the nineteenth century, more than a hundred years after the composer's death. The Crystal Palace performances were very different from anything that Handel would have known, and the manner of performance was affected by circumstances specific to the time and place – the concert hall, the orchestral and choral institutions and the audiences of 1859 could not have been forseen by Handel. In Unit 25 we shall investigate some of the musical differences between Handel's performances and those at the Crystal Palace. The differences were such that *Messiah* virtually sounded like a different piece of music. You may prefer either the nineteenth-century treatment or a more 'authentic' one that tries to recapture the sounds of Handel's performances, depending on your own musical tastes. However, there is a clear sense in which the promoters of the Crystal Palace performances 'got it wrong'. The Crystal Palace performances were not re-interpretations based on an understanding of *Messiah* in its original composer/audience context. As far as we know, none of those involved with the performances made any attempt to come to terms, factually or imaginatively, with this aspect of the work, nor did they wish to do so. Their rather grandiose image of the oratorio was based not on a performance tradition that stretched back a century to Handel's own performances in the 1740s and 1750s, but on a different tradition that had begun with Handel Festivals in the late eighteenth century. You should find the material in the present section, dealing with the original composer/

audience context of *Messiah*, useful when you come to make the comparisons in Unit 25, as well as being enjoyable study material in its own right.

The broad approach implicit in our 'composer and audience' theme involves reference to various types of evidence. Much of our evidence for the audience at the performances is necessarily rather impressionistic: no-one surveyed the audiences at Salzburg in 1771 or Paris in 1830 with questionnaires about socio-economic groupings, and we have to rely on letters, diaries and the like to gain a sense of the occasions concerned. On the 'composer' side of our theme, Berlioz's introduction to the programme note on the *Symphonie Fantastique* gives us an unusually explicit statement of general intentions. But what about the musical (as distinct from literary) evidence? What can we discover about the way a composer put the music down on paper, the way he prepared performances, the type and number of performers at his disposal? The television programme accompanying this unit investigates some of the materials relating to *Messiah* that can provide answers to these questions. This type of evidence is fundamental in defining the object that we know as 'Handel's Messiah'. The purpose of the television programme is therefore not merely to present material about *Messiah*, but to show how musical and historical documents yield specific information about the composition and first performances of a particular work.

3.2 MUSICAL FORMS AND STYLE IN *MESSIAH*

Handel's *Messiah* is a musical work for vocal soloists, chorus and orchestra. It was intended for concert performance, though in circumstances that were not exactly parallel to a modern concert performance. In contrast to the symphonies that you studied in the first part of the unit, our approach to the oratorio *genre* is radically affected by the fact that we have moved from purely instrumental pieces to a literature-based form: *Messiah* is constructed mainly from musical settings of literary texts. At a very basic level, therefore, the 'meaning' of the music lies with the messages conveyed by the words. In the case of *Messiah* (as also in the case of Handel's other oratorios) we can be sure that the composer expected the audience to pay attention to the text. The musical delivery of the words by singers was supplemented by the provision of a programme booklet giving the full text of the oratorio, which could be purchased by the audience and followed during the performance. Figure 6 reproduces, from the original word-book for Handel's first performances of *Messiah*, the texts of the movements that we shall be taking as our musical examples.

We shall be studying a sequence of seven short movements, and I shall ask you to follow them from the word-book, just as the original audience did. The first item illustrated, the chorus 'For unto us a child is born' is not included (though you will hear this movement in Unit 25): our extract begins with an instrumental movement (not mentioned in the word-book) named 'Pifa' by Handel, followed by the recitative 'There were shepherds abiding in the fields' and the succeeding movements up to and including the song 'Rejoice greatly'. Here are the movements, and the numbers by which I shall refer to them for convenience:

1 *Pifa* (orchestra alone)

2 *Recitative* 'There were shepherds'

3 *Recitative, accompany'd* 'And lo'

4 *Recitative* 'And the angel'

5 *Recitative, accompany'd* 'And suddenly'

6 *Chorus* 'Glory to God'

7 *Song* 'Rejoice greatly'

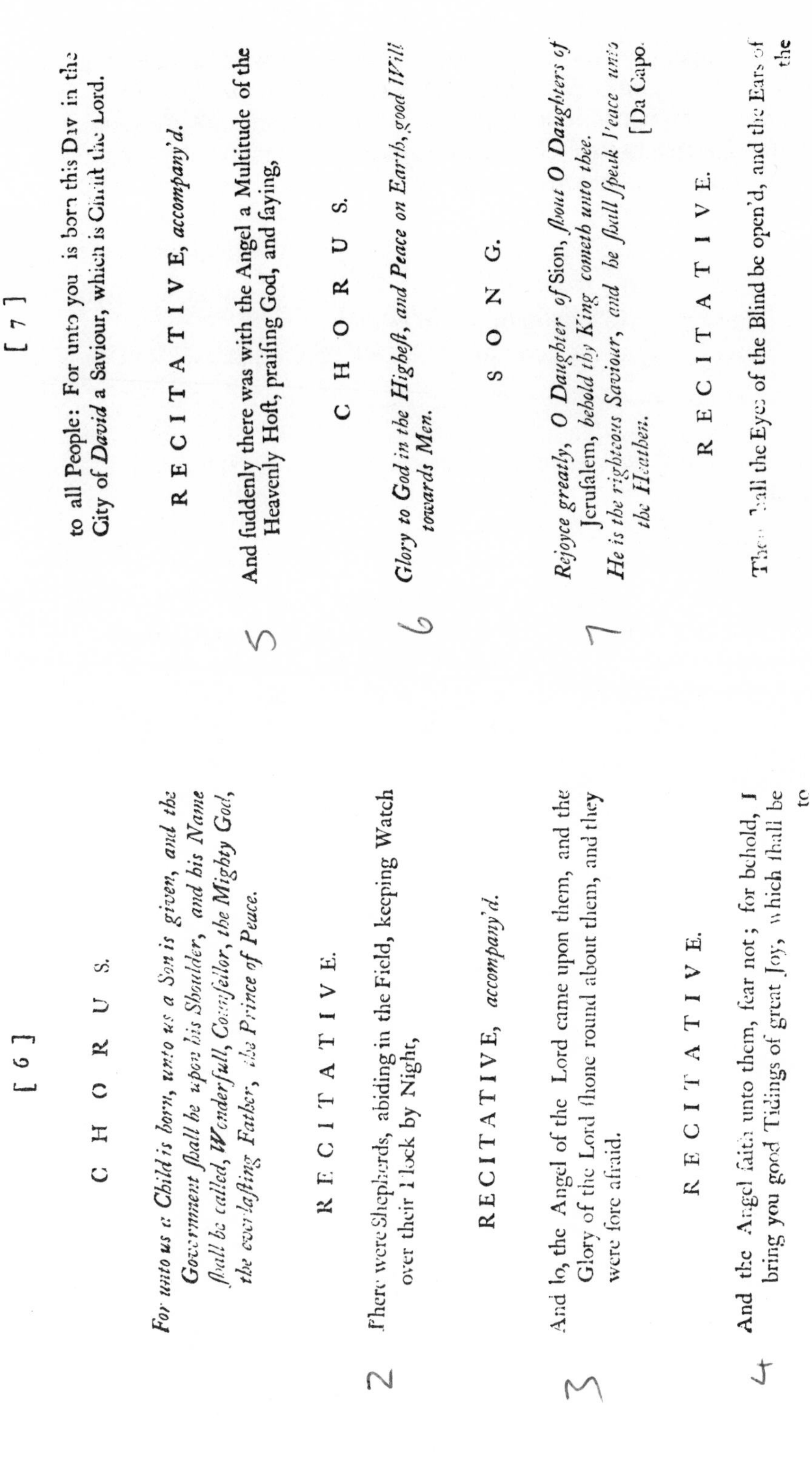

[6]

C H O R U S.

For unto us a Child is born, unto us a Son is given, and the Government ſhall be upon his Shoulder, and his Name ſhall be called, Wonderfull, Counſellor, the Mighty God, the everlaſting Father, the Prince of Peace.

R E C I T A T I V E.

2 There were Shepherds, abiding in the Field, keeping Watch over their Flock by Night,

RECITATIVE, *accompany'd.*

3 And lo, the Angel of the Lord came upon them, and the Glory of the Lord ſhone round about them, and they were ſore afraid.

R E C I T A T I V E.

4 And the Angel ſaith unto them, fear not; for behold, I bring you good Tidings of great Joy, which ſhall be to

[7]

to all People: For unto you is born this Day in the City of *David* a Saviour, which is Chriſt the Lord.

R E C I T A T I V E, *accompany'd.*

5 And ſuddenly there was with the Angel a Multitude of the Heavenly Hoſt, praiſing God, and ſaying,

C H O R U S.

6 *Glory to God in the Higheſt, and Peace on Earth, good Will towards Men.*

S O N G.

7 *Rejoyce greatly, O Daughter of* Sion, *ſhout O Daughters of* Jeruſalem, *behold thy King cometh unto thee.*
He is the righteous Saviour, and he ſhall ſpeak Peace unto the Heathen. [Da Capo.

R E C I T A T I V E.

Then ſhall the Eyes of the Blind be open'd, and the Ears of the

Figure 6 Two pages from an annotated Word-book for Messiah, *1742: (Photo: reproduced by permission of the British Library Board)*

Find the *Messiah* extract on cassette 3, side 2, band 6 now and listen to it once, following the text with figure 6. Movements 2–5 succeed one another very quickly. If you find no difficulty in following the words in their musical settings, go straight on to the exercise below. Otherwise, you may find it useful to play over the extract a few times to familiarize yourself with the music before proceeding.

Exercise

First, let us concentrate on the 'Pifa', No. 1. Play this movement again (twice, if it helps) and then answer the following question briefly:

Has the movement any descriptive function in relation to the words that follow?

My answer

Yes, it sets the mood and represents the pastoral scene of the shepherds looking after their sheep.

Further comments

Taking the extract as a whole, Handel wants to set up a contrast between the apparently peaceful routine of the shepherds and the sudden interruption provided by the appearance of the angels. He relied on certain conventional musical images that represented the countryside: his odd title seems to be a reference to the types of tunes traditionally associated with *Pifferari* – Italian Christmas waits who played primitive woodwind instruments. I would be very surprised if you had made the specific links between the countryside, shepherds' pipes and this type of music. Nevertheless, the peacefully-swinging rhythm and the static harmony convey the general mood well enough. When you listen to the movement again in a moment, notice particularly the long held notes in the bass part that contribute to this. It's worth remembering that the members of Handel's audience didn't have to guess what the *Pifa* represented, because they would almost certainly have read the words of the next recitative at the end of the chorus 'For unto us a child is born': rather, it was the case that the *Pifa* illustrated musically a scene that was already in their minds.

This movement is sometimes referred to as the 'Pastoral Symphony' – a name which is perhaps rather confusing in view of Beethoven's very different piece with the same name! The title is, however, quite correct in terms of the original meaning of the word 'symphony' as an instrumental piece within a primarily vocal *genre.*

Now let us turn our attention to the vocal movements.

Exercise

Each of movements 2–7 falls into one of the following categories:

1 An extended musical movement with prominent use of the orchestra. The musical development of the movement requires repetitions of the text.

2 Simple presentation of the text with no repetition of words. If the orchestra is used, it mainly provides simple accompaniment.

Listen to the complete extract again, with the words in front of you, and then write down the numbers of the movements that fall into each category.

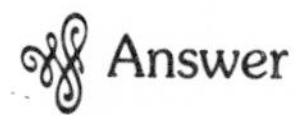

Answer

Category 1: Nos. 6 and 7

Category 2: Nos. 2, 3, 4 and 5

Supplementary question

You will notice that all of the movements in Category 2 are headed 'Recitative'. *Recitative* was developed originally for a musical *genre* other than oratorio. The style of No. 7 and the use of the word 'Symphony' to apply to No. 1 are also derived from the same musical *genre* (see section 2.1 on the last point). What *genre* am I referring to?

Answer

Opera

3.3 THE GENRE HISTORY BEHIND MESSIAH

The last answer brings us to the most important starting point for an understanding of *Messiah*. Historically, oratorio was an opera-derived *genre*, first developed in Italy during the early years of the seventeenth century. The name 'Oratorio' comes from the buildings in which the first examples were performed. 'Oratories' were buildings in which religious ceremonies or devotional performances took place: they were distinguished from churches in that the Mass, the principal religious service of the Roman tradition, was not necessarily celebrated there. Oratorios were dramatic presentations of a story using musical techniques derived from opera. A performance of *Rappresentatione di Anima, e di Corpo* (The Representation of the Soul and the Body), composed by Emilio Cavaliere, in the oratory of St. Philip Neri, Rome, in 1600 is generally taken to mark the beginning of the history of oratorio. Here the new operatic style was applied to a moralistic drama and, as you might guess from the title, the characters of the drama are allegorical. Intellect, Pleasure and a Guardian Angel try to exert their influence on the Soul and the Body, who eventually decide that the path to heaven is preferable to that to hell. The drama was staged and semi-acted, with dances at the end of each of the three parts or acts.

Allegorical stories provided one type of drama suitable for musical performance in an oratory. An obvious alternative lay with the dramatization of biblical stories, and the Old Testament supplied a good number of suitable incidents for treatment in the operatic style. A third possibility, which developed somewhat later, was the dramatization of incidents from the lives of saints. In general subsequent oratorios, although they used the musical techniques of opera, were not acted, and many scholars would include in their definition of an oratorio a statement to the effect that stage action is not characteristic of the form. This immediately removes a naturalistic element from oratorio, and leaves more to the listener's imagination to compensate for this; you may see something of a parallel in the contrast between drama presented on film and on the radio. In some circumstances this difference became diplomatically convenient. In many places in Italy theatres were closed during Lent, but oratorios were allowed: allowed, that is, provided they did not become too theatrical. In Protestant countries there was a certain puritan resistance to the theatre, and here again non-acted oratorio allowed everyone to enjoy the forbidden fruits of the operatic style with an easy conscience.

You will have noticed that, in my rough classification of oratorio subjects, I did not include the most obvious source for Christian drama, stories from the life of Christ. There was a particular problem here because of a reluctance to have Christ portrayed naturalistically by a mere human actor or singer. The understandable scruples on this point were gradually overcome, but in a tradition that had rather different origins from that of the Italian oratorio. In parts of Lutheran Germany it became the practice to present the gospel narrative of Christ's passion and death in music during Holy Week. This was done in the context of a church service, as an elevated presentation of the appropriate gospel reading for that particular service. (The Italian oratorios, by contrast, were of the nature of popular 'performances', even though in a consecrated building.) It is significant that when Heinrich Schütz published a musical setting of the narrative of the resurrection story in 1623, he set the words of Christ to be sung by two voices. Schütz had been greatly influenced by the Italian operatic style, and in a preface he almost apologized for setting words in this way, suggesting that one of the voice parts might be played on an instrument instead. By the first decade of the eighteenth century, German composers were treating the passion story in the oratorio style, with recitatives and arias (songs) for the leading characters, including Christ.

Handel's oratorios

George Frideric Handel (1685–1759) received his earliest musical education in Halle, the German town of his birth. He developed an interest in opera, which took him first to a job in the opera house at Hamburg and then to Italy. It was in Italy that he composed his first oratorios, one allegorical, *Il Trionfo del Tempo* ('The Triumph of Time' 1707), and one narrative, *Oratorio per la Resurrezione* ('The Resurrection' 1708). Little is known about the performance of the first, though it probably took place in Rome, where the second one was performed in 1708. Handel's patron, Marquis Francesco Ruspoli, spared no expense for *La Resurrezione*, which was performed at his palace with an elaborate stage setting but no acting: the characters represented in the oratorio were an Angel, Mary Magdalene, Cleophas, St. John and Lucifer.

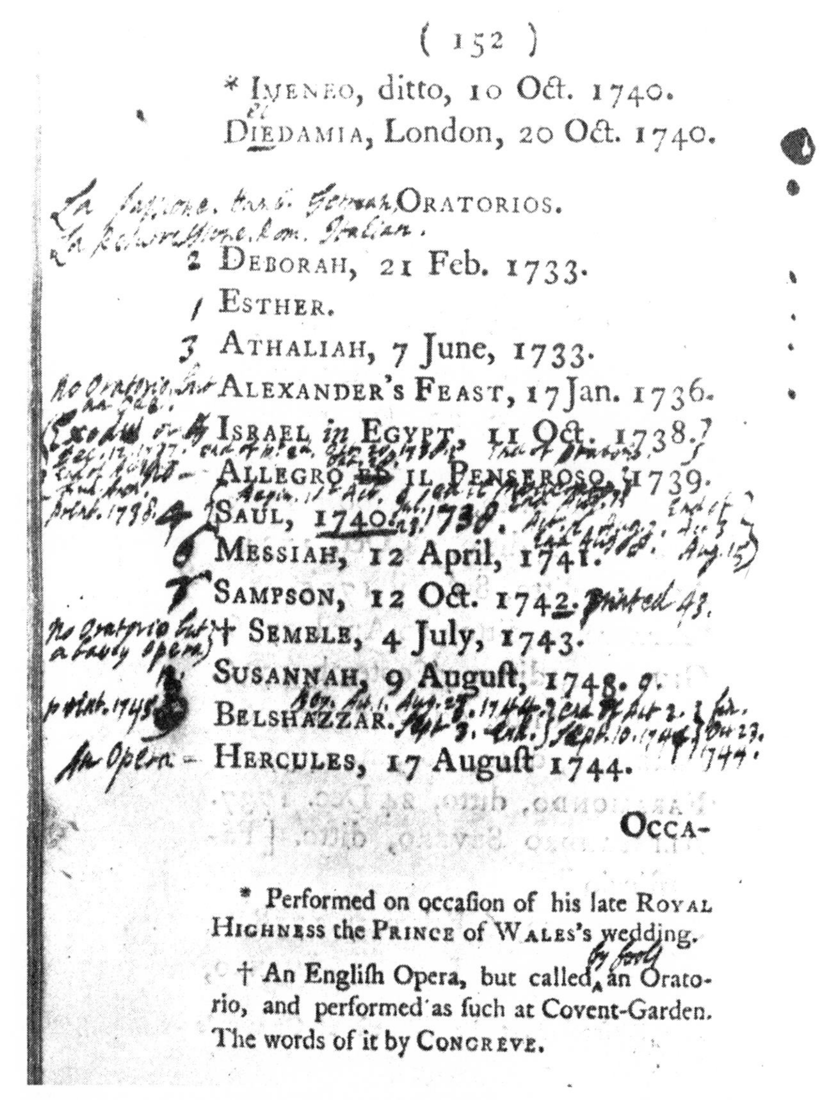

(152)

* Imeneo, ditto, 10 Oct. 1740.
Diedamia, London, 20 Oct. 1740.

ORATORIOS.

Deborah, 21 Feb. 1733.
Esther.
Athaliah, 7 June, 1733.
Alexander's Feast, 17 Jan. 1736.
Israel in Egypt, 11 Oct. 1738.
Allegro ed il Penseroso, 1739.
Saul, 1740.
Messiah, 12 April, 1741.
Sampson, 12 Oct. 1742.
† Semele, 4 July, 1743.
Susannah, 9 Auguſt, 1743.
Belshazzar.
Hercules, 17 Auguſt 1744.

Occa-

* Performed on occaſion of his late Royal Highness the Prince of Wales's wedding.

† An Engliſh Opera, but called an Oratorio, and performed as ſuch at Covent-Garden. The words of it by Congreve.

Figure 7 A page from Jennens's annotated copy of Mainwaring's biography of Handel: (Photo: reproduced in 'Charles Jennens' Marginalia to Mainwaring's Life of Handel' by Winton Dean, Music and Letters, *1972; by courtesy of Robin Golding)*

Handel left Italy in 1710. Following an initial visit to London, he returned there again in 1712 and spent the rest of his professional life in England. In 1716 he composed a German Passion-oratorio, apparently for performace in Hamburg, but it is doubtful that Handel travelled over for the performance. Just as his first Italian oratorios had been produced semi-privately for an aristocratic patron, so his first English oratorio *Esther* (based on the Old Testament story) was written for a private performance arranged by James Brydges, Earl of Carnarvon, better known by his later title of the Duke of Chandos. Oratorios were, as they continued to be for some years, occasional incidents in Handel's life: his real musical career was as a composer of Italian operas.

In later years, the musical basis of Handel's career changed from (acted) Italian operas to (non-acted) oratorio-type works in English. His career nevertheless remained in the theatre, where he gave most of his performances of oratorios as well as operas. The introduction of *Esther* into his theatre season in 1732 amidst his normal run of Italian operas came about almost by accident, but it proved popular and in subsequent years Handel, hard pressed by a rival opera company, developed English works to diversify his programmes. A rather confused period during which Handel seemed uncertain about the future direction of his career ended with him leaving London to give a series of performances in Dublin during 1741–2. After his return to London he never gave another opera performance. In the following ten years, before blindness limited his activities, Handel composed a series of large-scale English works for theatre performance. Along with oratorios proper, there were some based on secular (i.e. non-religious) stories, but composed in the same style and performed in the same way as the oratorios. Not surprisingly, all of these works are sometimes lumped together as 'Handel's oratorios', and the blurring of terminology goes back a long time. Charles Jennens (1700–73), one of Handel's librettists, annotated a list of Handel's oratorios published soon after the composer's death. As you can see (figure 7) he wrote 'No Oratorio, but an Ode' against *Alexander's Feast*, 'No' against *L'Allegro*, 'No Oratorio but a baudy opera' against *Semele* and 'An Opera' against *Hercules* (neither *Semele* nor *Hercules* were acted). The remaining works are all based on biblical stories, and Jennens added Handel's German setting of the Passion and his Italian Resurrection oratorio to the list. Jennens obviously followed a more fastidious definition of 'oratorio' than the compiler of the list.

The rather complicated genre history behind Handel's *Messiah* has inevitably required some rather concentrated explanation. You don't need to remember all of the details, but it is desirable to understand the background in general terms before proceeding to the next sections. Instead of an exercise, therefore, I am now going to ask you to re-read section 3.3 before proceeding.

3.4 *MESSIAH* AS AN EXAMPLE OF DRAMATIC MUSICAL STYLE

Exercise

Play the complete extract through again, following the words as before, and then answer the following questions:

1 In what ways could you describe the music as 'dramatic'? How does the music reflect the dramatic situations outlined by the words?

2 In what way does the extract differ from what you would expect of an opera (i.e. a play sung throughout to music)? Answer in a short paragraph.

My answers (longer than I would expect yours to be)

1 I mentioned earlier that the extract uses the *forms* of opera – instrumental symphony, recitative, aria (or, as here, 'Song'). Beyond this we can say:

(a) That the music employs dramatic contrasts. The peace of the shepherds is broken by the appearance of the angel; the chorus of angels breaks out behind the soloist with quite theatrical effect. Within the chorus there is the contrast between 'Glory to God in the highest' (high voices) and 'and peace on earth' (low voices). Similarly, within 'Rejoice greatly' there is a contrast at 'he shall speak peace'.

(b) That there is some operatic-style characterization of persons and situations. The high voice is Nos. 2–5 may be taken to represent the angel, the chorus to represent the angel host. No. 7 portrays the reaction to the news given by the chorus, the soloist presumably acting as a spokesperson for a wider community, following a fairly frequently encountered dramatic convention.

(c) That the orchestral accompaniment reinforces the theatrical effect with various descriptive or pictorial touches. We noted the 'pastoral' element in the *Pifa* earlier: you might also have noticed the 'wing-flapping' in the accompanied recitatives – gently at first in 'And lo' as the solo angel appears, and then more busily in 'And suddenly' as the angel host gathers. At the end of the chorus, the orchestral postlude suggests the gradual disappearance of the angels.

2 On the other hand, the extract isn't operatic because the story is narrated, not enacted. The soprano soloist, as well as incidentally impersonating the angel, also has to tell the story. The chorus appear 'in character' as the angel host, but the soloist for 'Rejoice greatly' does not appear as a named character. The soprano soloist, in fact, has to change from being a representative of the angels to a representative of humanity.

Your answer was probably not as detailed as mine, but if you noted at least some of these points, well done. I suggest that you now play the extract one last time, with my comments in mind, before proceeding.

 Further comment and question

The presentation of the story in *Messiah* is not typical of Handel's oratorios as a whole. In his oratorio *Samson*, composed immediately after *Messiah*, one singer represented Samson, another Delilah, and so on: most of Handel's oratorios have a cast in the same way as his operas, and his librettists used biblical stories as the framework for theatrical dramas, with newly-written texts. In *Messiah*, however, the story is told in narrative form, relying wholly on passages selected from the Bible, and Handel illustrates events rather than characters. There is no cast as such.

Referring back to the material in section 3.2, can you suggest a reason for the unusual manner of presentation in *Messiah*?

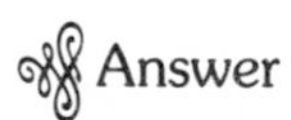 Answer

The subject of the oratorio, dealing with Christ's life, was a sensitive one that needed special treatment if it was to be accepted.

3.5 *MESSIAH* AND THE AUDIENCE

Handel composed *Messiah* in London during August and September 1741, and followed it immediately with the composition of *Samson* during September–October. This was in line with his normal habit in his later years of writing a couple of works at that time of year in readiness for the new season of oratorios. As far as we can tell from the music, he composed the oratorios just as if he were expecting a normal season at the London theatre to follow. In November, however, he packed his bags and left for Dublin, where he gave a very successful season of performances – mainly English odes and oratorios, but with one Italian work, his opera *Imeneo* in a concert performance. Of the newly-composed works, he did not perform *Samson* at all (probably because it demanded more ambitious resources than were available to him) and left *Messiah* until the very end of his run of performances. It was not given as an item in Handel's repertory performances, but as an extra charity event at the end. Even so, *Messiah* was

Figure 8 First page of Messiah *autograph: (Photo: reproduced by permission of the British Library Board)*

given in the same concert hall (the 'New Music Hall') as his other performances and, as far as we can tell, to the same type of audience as had attended the rest of his series. Following Handel's return to London, he gave a season of oratorio performances at Covent Garden Theatre during February and March in 1743, incorporating three performances of *Messiah* towards the end of the run. *Messiah* was therefore first performed in Dublin in April 1742, and in London in March 1743.

The audiences for Handel's oratorios in Dublin and London were probably drawn from much the same areas of society, mainly the more affluent sections of the middle classes. It seems that oratorios did not have quite the same social *cachet* as opera. At the height of the popularity of Italian opera in London, around 1720, the subscribers to Handel's opera company had included seven Dukes, twelve Earls, four Viscounts and six Lords, but there is no evidence that he attracted such a dazzling array to his oratorios twenty years later. The subscription lists for publications of his music in the late 1730s reflect some support from the Royal Family, but otherwise there are only a couple of Earls and a handful of Countesses. In his later years Handel appears to have had a small but enthusiastic group of noble supporters, but these cannot have formed more than a small part of his audience. Subscription prices, although not as high as for the operas, assumed a modest affluence: in London in 1743 a six guinea subscription to the oratorios entitled you to three seats in a theatre box for six performances. 'On the door' gallery tickets were at more or less the same levels as they had been for the operas. Some interesting sidelights on the Dublin audience (for whom Handel's performances were something of a novelty) are revealed by references in advertisements to an extra room hired for the convenience of waiting footmen, and by requests that the gentlemen should come without swords and the ladies without hoops (i.e. hooped dresses) so that there would be room for a large audience.

The reactions of the Dublin and London audiences to *Messiah* were, however, very different. This can partly be accounted for by the way the work was promoted, but mainly we must look to the work itself for an explanation.

Exercise

Read the six extracts given below. These, of course, are historical documents and, strictly speaking, in interpreting them you should go through the critical processes described in Unit 2; however, for the purposes of this exercise, you can take it that these documents are straightforward and reliable. Three refer to Handel' s performances of *Messiah* in Dublin, three to the first performance in London. Look also at the advertisement for the first London performance (figure 9).

Compare the reception that *Messiah* received in the two cities, and explain the reason for the work's controversial reception in London.

From Faulkner's 'Dublin Journal', 10 April 1742

Yesterday Mr Handel's new Grand Sacred Oratorio, called, the MESSIAH, was rehearsed... to a most Grand, Polite and crouded Audience; and was performed so well, that it gave universal Satisfaction to all present; and was allowed by the greatest Judges to be the finest Composition of Musick that ever was heard, and the sacred Words as properly adapted for the Occasion.

From Faulkner's 'Dublin Journal', 17 April 1742

On Tuesday last [the 13th] Mr Handel's Sacred Grand Oratorio, the MESSIAH, was performed at the New Musick-Hall in Fishamble-street; the best Judges allowed it to be the most finished piece of Musick. Words are wanting to express the exquisite Delight it afforded to the admiring Audience. The Sublime, the Grand, and the Tender, adapted to the most elevated, majestick and moving Words, conspired to transport and charm the ravished Heart and Ear. It is but Justice to Mr Handel, that the World should know, he generously gave the Money arising from this Grand Performance, to be equally shared by the Society for relieving Prisoners, the Charitable Infirmary, and Mercer's Hospital, for which they will ever gratefully remember his Name;... There were about 700 People in the Room, and the Sum collected for that Noble and Pious Charity amounted to about 400 l. [£] out of which 127 l. goes to each of the three great and pious Charities.

Letter: Handel to Jennens, 9 September 1742

It was indeed Your humble Servant which intended You a visit in my way from Ireland to London, for I certainly could have given You a better account by word of mouth, as by writing, how well Your *Messiah was recieved in that Country, yet as a Noble Lord, and no less than the Bishop of Elphim (a Nobleman very learned in Musick) has given his Observation in writing of this Oratorio, I send you here annexed the Contents of it in his own words.

[enclosure]

As Mr Handel in his oratorio's greatly excells all other Composers I am acquainted with, So in the famous one, called The Messiah he seems to have excell'd himself. The whole is beyond any thing I had a notion of till I Read and heard it. It Seems to be a Species of Musick different from any other, and this is particulary remarkable of it. That tho' the Composition is very Masterly and artificial, yet the Harmony is So great and open, as to please all who have Ears and will hear, learned and unlearn'd... [another] reason for the Superior Excellence of this piece, 'Tis this there is no Dialogue. In every Drame there must a great deal and often broken into very Short Speeches and Answers. If these be flat and insipid, they move laughter or Contempt...'

**The selection of the text for* Messiah *had been made for Handel by Charles Jennens.*

Letter: Jennens to Edward Holdsworth, 21 February 1742

What adds to my chagrin is, that if he [Handel] makes his Oratorio ever so perfect, there is a clamour about Town, said to arise from the B's against performing it. This may occasion some enlargement of the Preface.

The 'Universal Spectator' (a London newspaper) 19 March 1743

Sir,
... My... Purpose... is to consider, and, if possible, induce others to consider, the Impropriety of *Oratorios*, as they are now perform'd. An *Oratorio* either is an *Act of Religion*, or it is not; if it is, I ask if the *Playhouse* is a fit Temple to perform it in, or a Company of *Players* fit *Ministers of God's Word*, for in that Case such they are made.

In the other Case, if it is not perform'd as an *Act of Religion*, but for *Diversion and Amusement* only (and indeed I believe few or none go to an *Oratorio* out of *Devotion*), what a *Prophanation* of God's name and Word is this, to make so light Use of them?... David said, *How can we sing the Lord's Song in a strange Land*; but sure he would have thought it much stranger to have heard it sung in a *Playhouse*.

But it seems the *Old Testament* is not to be prophan'd alone nor *God* by the *Name* of *Jehovah* only, but the *New* must be join'd with it, and *God* by the most *sacred* the most *merciful Name*, of *Messiah*; for I'm inform'd that an Oratorio call'd by that Name has already been perform'd in *Ireland*, and is soon is to be perform'd here: What the Piece itself is, I know not, and therefore shall say nothing about it; but I must again ask, If the *Place* and *Performers* are fit?

Philalethes*

Letter, Jennens to Holdsworth, 24 March 1743

... Messiah was perform'd last night, & will be again tomorrow, notwithstanding the clamour rais'd against it, which has only occasion'd it's being advertis'd without its Name; a Farce which gives me as much of offence as any thing relating to the performance can give the Bs. & other squeamish People. Tis after all, in the main, a fine Composition, notwithstanding some weak parts, which he was too idle & too obstinate to retouch, tho' I us'd great importunity to perswade him to it.

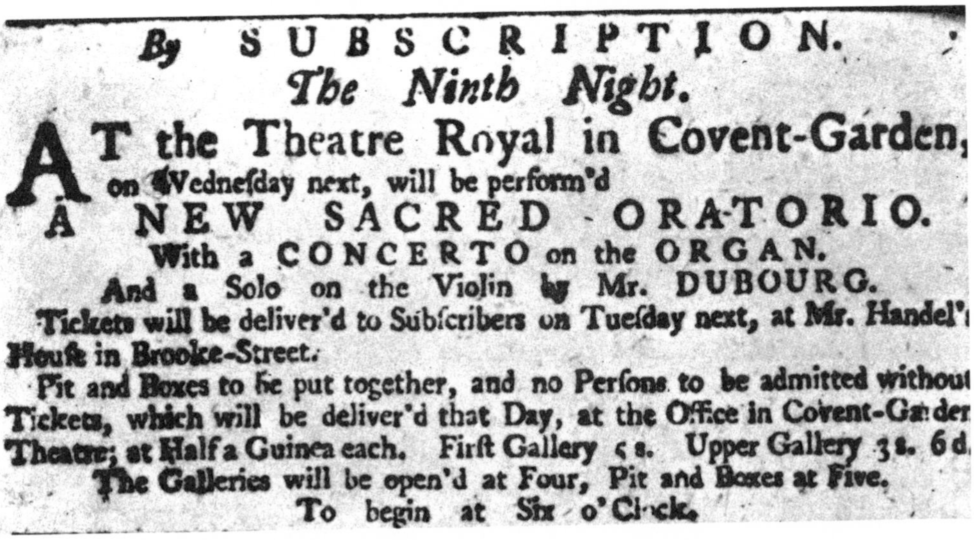

By SUBSCRIPTION.
The Ninth Night.
AT the Theatre Royal in Covent-Garden, on Wedneſday next, will be perform'd
A NEW SACRED ORATORIO.
With a CONCERTO on the ORGAN.
And a Solo on the Violin by Mr. DUBOURG.
Tickets will be deliver'd to Subſcribers on Tueſday next, at Mr. Handel's Houſe in Brooke-Street.
Pit and Boxes to be put together, and no Perſons to be admitted without Tickets, which will be deliver'd that Day, at the Office in Covent-Garden Theatre, at Half a Guinea each. Firſt Gallery 5 s. Upper Gallery 3 s. 6 d.
The Galleries will be open'd at Four, Pit and Boxes at Five.
To begin at Six o'Clock.

Figure 9 Advertisement for first London performance of Messiah, Daily Advertiser, *19 March 1743: (Photo: reproduced by permission of the British Library Board)*

'Philalethes' was a pseudonym: the identity of the author of the letter is unknown.

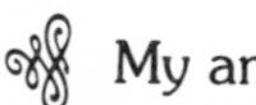
My answer

Messiah was received with enthusiasm in Dublin. It was approved at the public rehearsal and, significantly, the subject was linked to the fact that it was to be performed for charity. The Bishop of Elphim not only approved of the performance, but was enthusiastic about the application of operatic techniques: the oratorio has recitatives in place of the 'Flat and insipid' dialogue of a spoken drama.

In London, the reception of *Messiah* was marred by a 'clamour' raised against it even before the first performance. (We do not know who the 'B's' were that Jennens refers to: it has been suggested that he meant either Bishops or Brethren/ Methodists.) The argument put forward in the newspapers (on the same day as the first performance was advertised) is that the subject of the oratorio was unsuitable for performance in a theatre, which was a place of public entertainment. (In a later letter, Jennens himself referred to *Messiah* as 'A fine entertainment'.) Handel was apparently so anxious about the work's reception that he dared not advertise the performance as 'Messiah', but instead chose to call it 'The Sacred Oratorio'.

Further comments

Obviously the unusual nature of this particular oratorio explains its controversial reception in London. A verse countering the arguments of 'Philalethes' appeared in the newspapers soon after the last performance of *Messiah* in 1743:

From 'The Daily Advertiser', 31 March 1743

> Wrote extempore by a Gentleman, on reading the *Universal Spectator.*
> *On Mr* HANDEL'S *new* ORATORIO,
> *perform'd at the Theatre Royal in Covent Garden.*
>
> Cease, Zealots, cease to blame these Heav'nly Lays,
> For Seraphs fit to sing Messiah's Praise!
> Not, for your trivial Argument, assign,
> 'The Theatre not fit for praise Divine'.
>
> These hallow'd Lays to Musick give new Grace,
> To Virtue Awe, and sanctify the Place;
> To Harmony, like his, Celestial Pow'r is giv'n,
> T'exalt the Soul from Earth, and make, of Hell, a Heav'n.

This attracted a rebuttal from 'Philalethes' and, although it is difficult to measure the strength of feeling on both sides, the general impression left by the episode is that the controversy over *Messiah* was not good for Handel's reputation. It was not good for Handel himself, who suffered a 'paralytic disorder' almost certainly as a result of the tensions which accompanied the end of his oratorio season. (Handel was fifty-eight years old.)

We know very little about Handel's own attitude to *Messiah* and the controversy in 1743: unlike Queen Victoria, he was not the sort of person to keep a diary recording his feelings and reactions to events. The only direct evidence is an anecdote recorded nearly forty years later.

> Some days after the first exhibition of the same divine oratorio (*Messiah*), Handel came to pay his respect to Lord Kinnoull, with whom he was particularly acquainted. His lordship, as was natural, paid him some compliments on the noble entertainment which he had lately given the town. 'My Lord', said Handel, 'I should be sorry if I only entertained them, I wish to make them better'. (Letter from James Beattie to the Reverend Dr. Laing, Aberdeen, 25 May 1780)

This remark sounds uncharacteristically sententious when compared with the way that Handel expressed himself on various subjects in his letters, though it fits well enough with the image that Handel's personality acquired soon after his death. We might perhaps dismiss the anecdote as inadequate evidence. Nevertheless, it is a fact that Thomas Hay, 8th Earl of Kinnoull, was in London in 1743 and may have been reporting as correctly as his memory allowed. If Handel's reported words are correct, it sounds as if he was on the defensive after the London *Messiah* controversy.

Not surprisingly, Handel was circumspect about performing *Messiah* again. He gave no performances in 1744, a couple in 1745 and then no more until a single performance in 1749. The change in *Messiah's* fortunes came when circumstances led Handel to perform the oratorio somewhere other than in the theatre, the scene of 'fine Entertainments'. In 1749 he became involved with a charitable institution, the 'Society for the Maintenance and Education of Exposed and Deserted Young Children' (better known informally as the 'Foundling Hospital'), which was trying to complete an ambitious residential building at Lamb's Conduit Fields on the outskirts of London. In 1750 he presented the Hospital with an organ and offered a performance of *Messiah* in the Chapel of the Hospital in aid of the charity. About a thousand people turned up, more than the Chapel could hold, and a second performance had to be arranged. In each subsequent year until his death in 1759 Handel gave *Messiah* as the last performance of his oratorio season at Covent Garden Theatre and then repeated the performance with one or two presentations at the Foundling Hospital. Thus, in the end, he gave more performances of *Messiah* than of any other oratorio, and by 1759 the work was established as a popular favourite. A curious fact is that, once established by the charity performances in the Foundling Hospital Chapel, *Messiah* never again seems to have faced censure in the theatre: the popularity of the Foundling Hospital performances was accompanied by acceptance for the work in general. It may well be that a change in public taste was involved as well, and that audiences going to Handel's oratorios in the 1750s were more seriously disposed than those in 1743. Certainly it is true that Handel's oratorios were being regarded as 'religious' works by the end of the eighteenth century in a way that would have surprised the composer when he presented his first theatre performance of *Esther* in 1732.

Messiah gives us a particularly good example of the interaction of the three influences that were outlined in the introduction to this unit. It was written against the background of previous compositions in the oratorio *genre*, yet adapted to particular conditions – those that would attract an audience to the London theatres. Because of the individual subject of *Messiah*, Handel had to treat it in a certain way to make it acceptable: even so, he misjudged the opposition that was likely to be raised against it. His audience apparently took to the work unreservedly only when it was transferred to performance in a sacred building – a building, ironically, somewhat comparable to the 'oratories' of Italy that had given the musical *genre* its name.

REFERENCES

Berlioz, H. (1972) *Symphonie Fantastique*, ed. Nicholas Temperley, Kassel, Basel, Tours.

Cairns, D. (1977) *The Memoirs of Hector Berlioz*, Gollancz.

Landon, H.C.R. (1970) *Beethoven: A Documentary Study*, Thames and Hudson.

SCORE OF SCHUMANN'S 'AVEU'

ACKNOWLEDGEMENT

Grateful acknowledgement is made to the sources for material used in these units: 'Over the Rainbow', E. Y. Harburg and H. Arlen, © 1938, 1939 (renewed 1966, 1967) Metro-Goldwyn-Mayer Inc. All Rights Controlled and Administered by CBS Feist Catalog Inc. Reproduced by permission of Belwin Mills Music Limited, 250 Purley Way, Croydon, Surrey; 'Day Trip to Bangor', Fiddler's Dram, Composer Debbie Cook, Intersong Music Ltd.